Contents

Perspective

Maps present information about
the world in a simple, visual way.
This is a bedroom from the perspective
of a person standing in it.

This is the same room from above. It's easier to get a clear perspective on a space when you take an aerial view.

Colour me in!

My Room

Draw an aerial view
of the room you're in.

Reading Maps

N

A compass tells
you which way
is north.

The map's key will tell you
what the symbols, such as
points, lines, patterns
and colours mean.

The scale tells you how
much area the map covers.
On a 1:50,000 scale map,
for example, 1 cm=0.5 km.

The grid of a map helps
people locate places. On a
small-scale map, the grid
is usually made of numbered
latitude and longitude lines.
The intersection of latitude
and longitude lines are
called co-ordinates and help
identify where places can
be found on the map.

C
3

On larger-scale maps, the grid is
sometimes divided into numbers
and letters. The map's index might
list a museum being in grid square
'C3', indicating that you can find
it in the box where column C and
row 3 intersect.

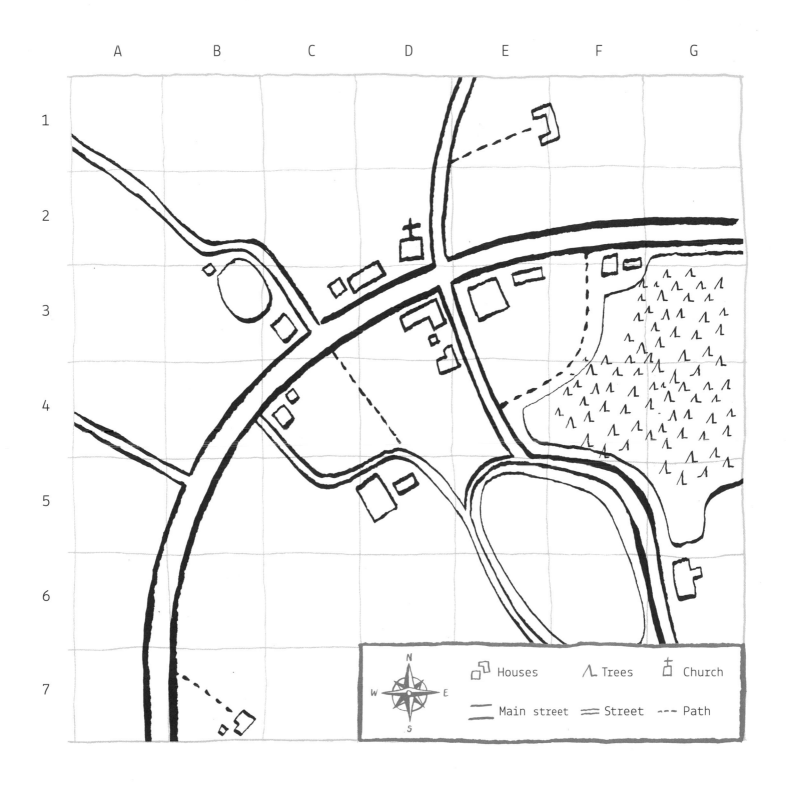

My Neighbourhood

Draw a map of your own
town or neighbourhood.

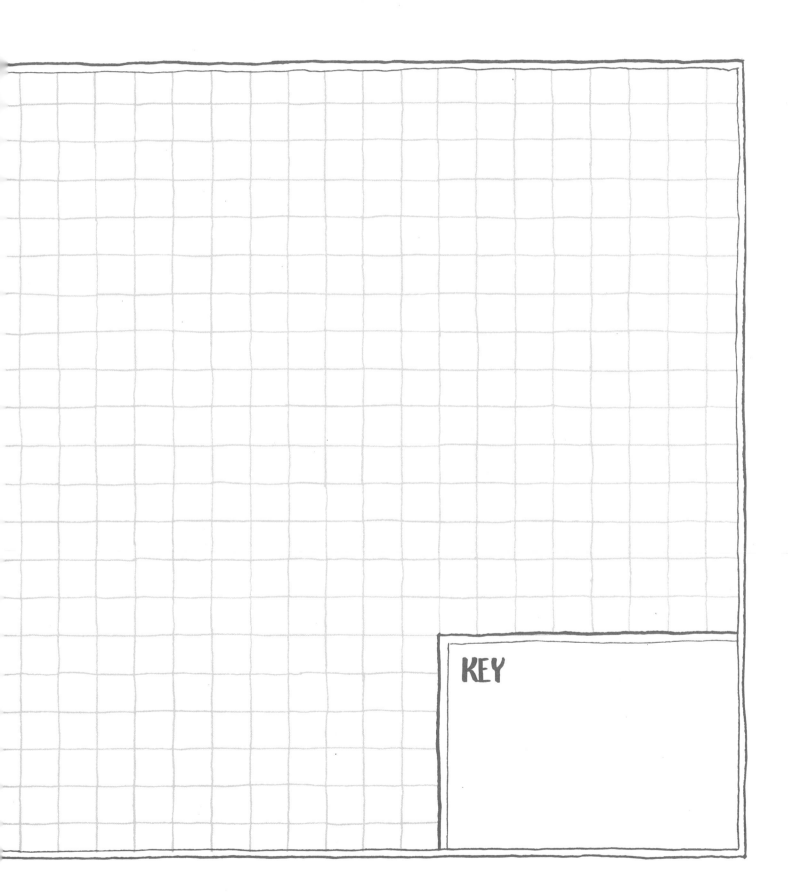

KEY

Street Sense

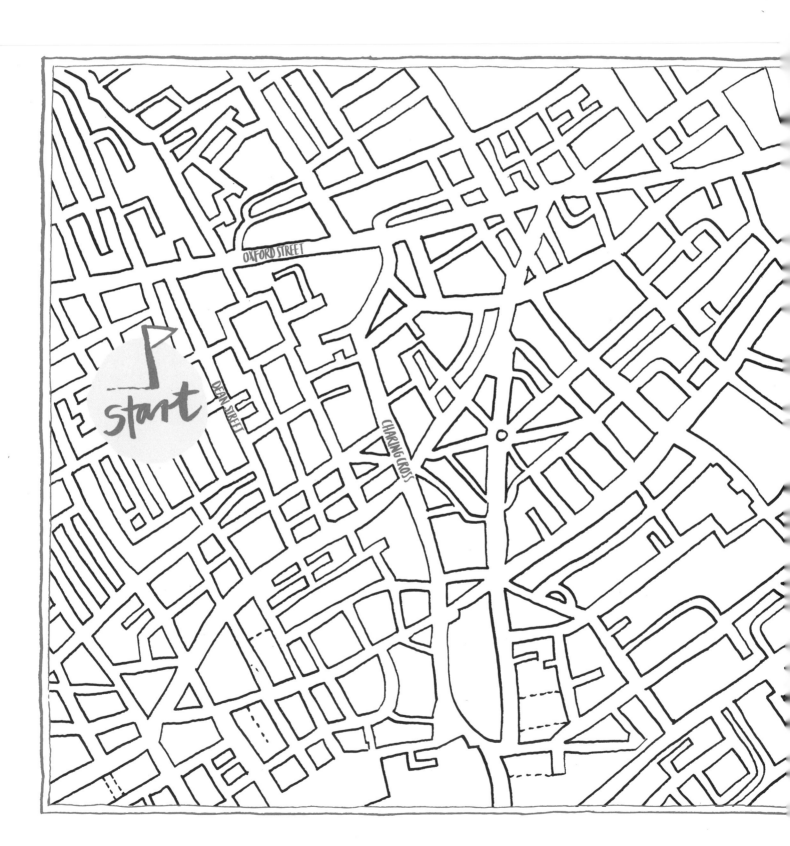

Start

OXFORD STREET

DEAN STREET

CHARING CROSS

Big cities can be difficult to navigate.
Can you find out how to get from
Dean Street to the corner of Farringdon Road
and Holborn in London?

If you were cycling, you might want a more scenic route.
Can you pick your way through the back streets without
adding too much time to your journey?

Some big cities are divided into districts,
to make it easier to navigate. In Paris,
the districts are numbered, and they wrap
around from the centre like a snail.

Can you colour the districts in four
colours, making sure that districts
in the same colour don't touch?

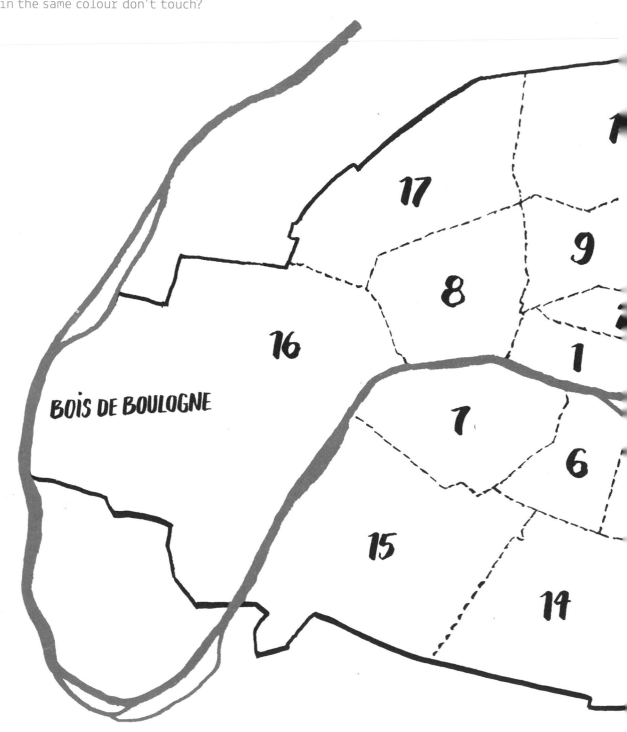

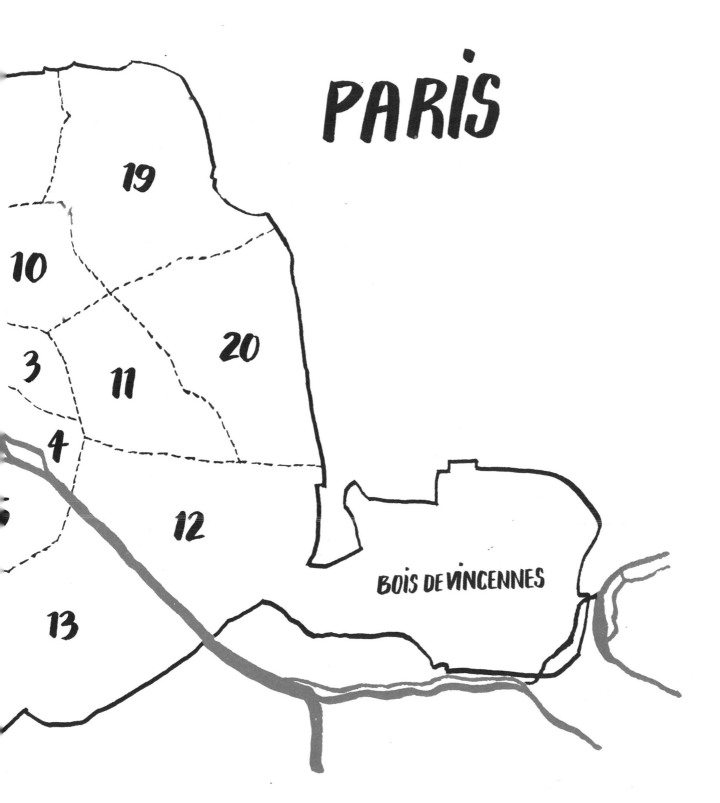

Underground

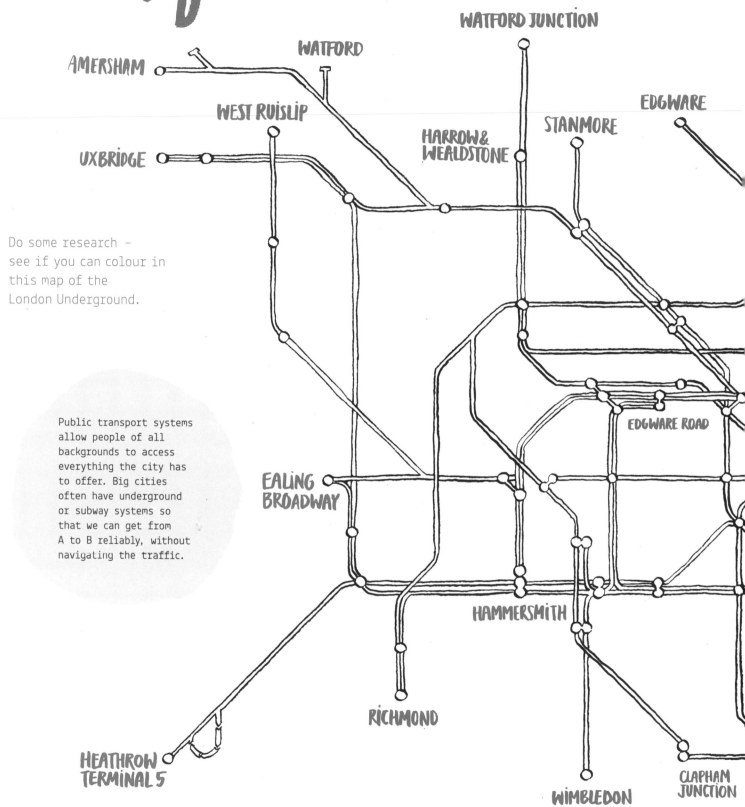

Do some research –
see if you can colour in
this map of the
London Underground.

Public transport systems
allow people of all
backgrounds to access
everything the city has
to offer. Big cities
often have underground
or subway systems so
that we can get from
A to B reliably, without
navigating the traffic.

AMERSHAM

WATFORD

WATFORD JUNCTION

WEST RUISLIP

EDGWARE

STANMORE

HARROW &
WEALDSTONE

UXBRIDGE

EDGWARE ROAD

EALING
BROADWAY

HAMMERSMITH

RICHMOND

HEATHROW
TERMINAL 5

WIMBLEDON

CLAPHAM
JUNCTION

MORDEN

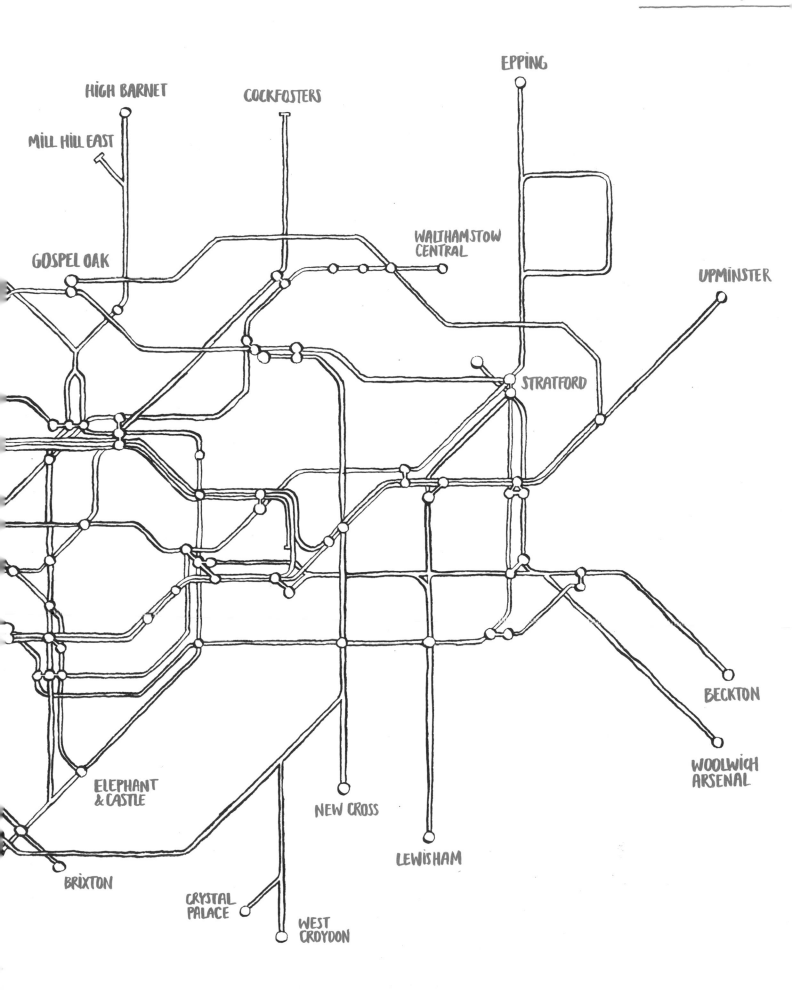

Tokyo Metro

The Tokyo Metro links with overground lines to reach deep into the city's suburbs, and bring commuters into town at super speeds.

Sometimes trains are so crowded that attendants need to push riders onto the subway cars so that the doors can close.

Colour me in!

City Map

Draw a map of a big city.
Mark the main roads and the
following landmarks:

4 post offices   1 river
6 museums   2 parks
8 churches   3 bridges   What transport links connect
3 railway stations   3 libraries   the various parts of the city?

KEY

Getting around

There are lots of ways to get around a city:

Cable car

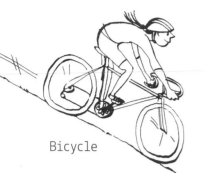
Bicycle

Bus

Car

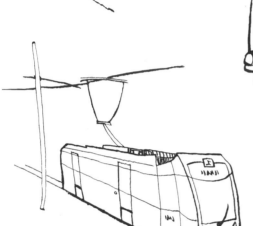
Tram

Train

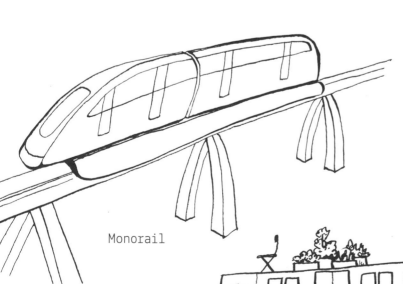
Monorail

On foot

Canal boat

Can you design a brand
new mode of transport
for your city?

Cities of the World

These blocks of colour represent the geographical size of some of the world's major cities.

1 square = 100 km²

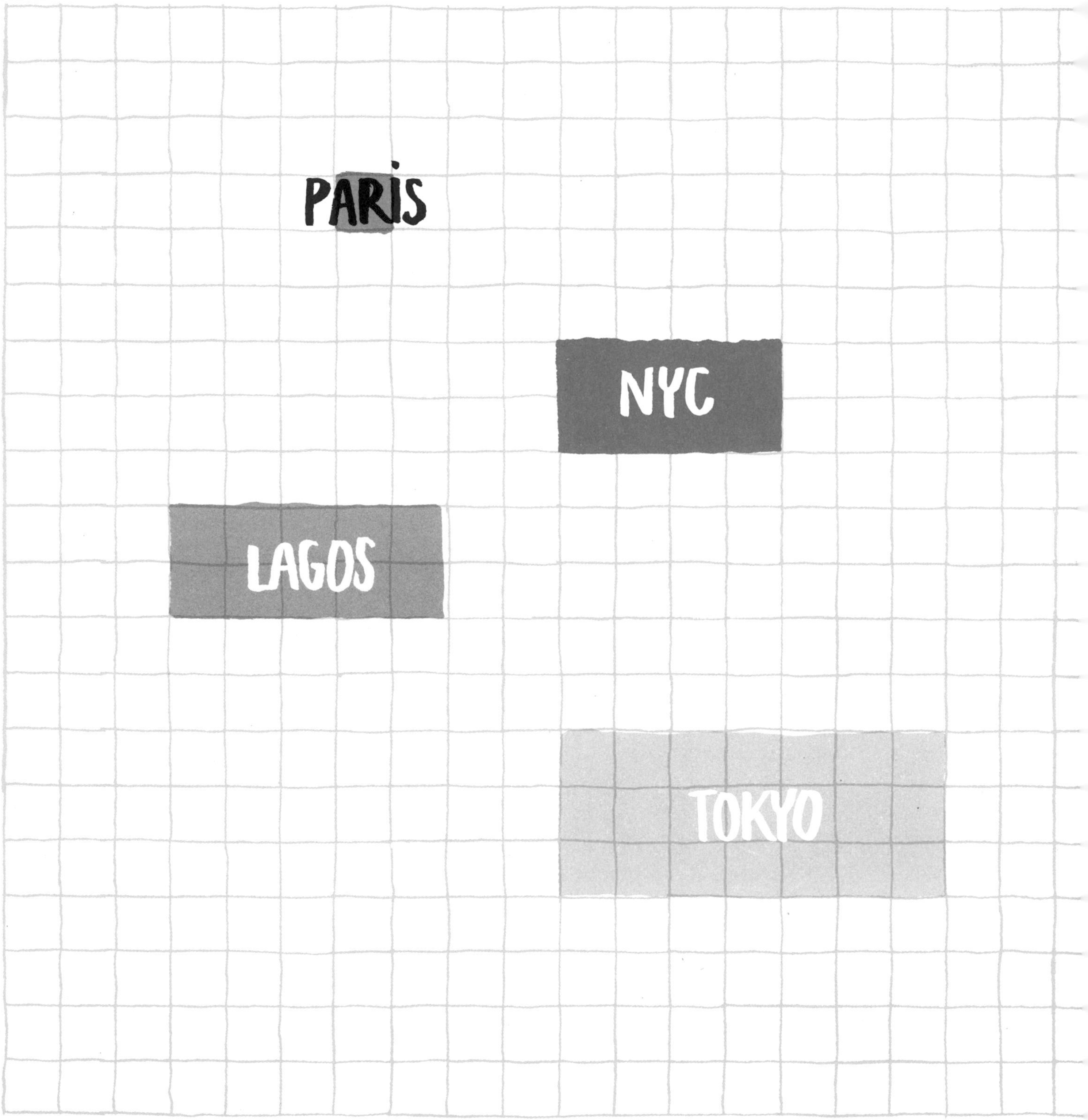

PARIS

NYC

LAGOS

TOKYO

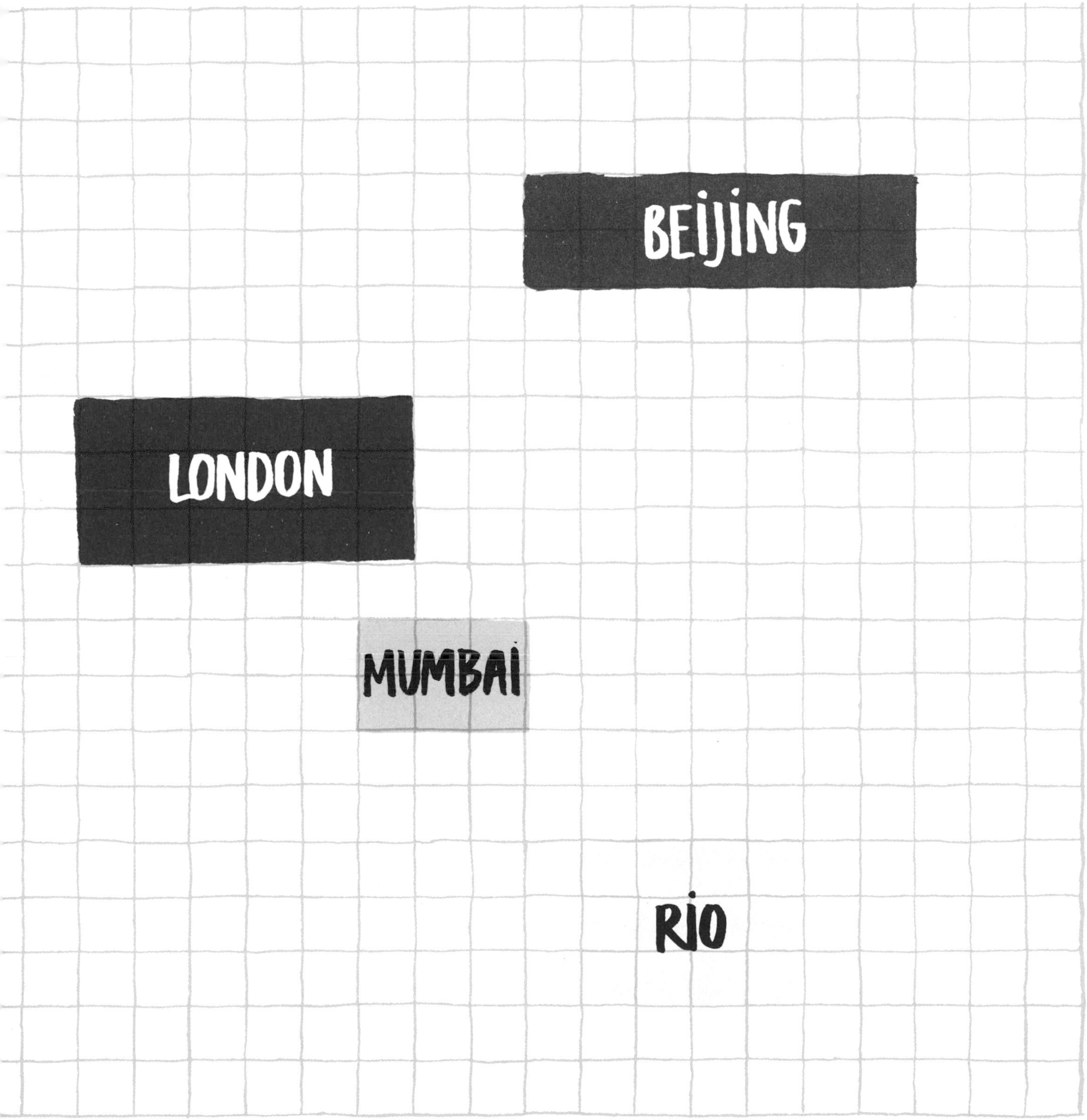

BEIJING

LONDON

MUMBAI

RIO

Populations

How do the cities' population size compare to their geographical size? Colour in this grid so that

1 square = 1 million people

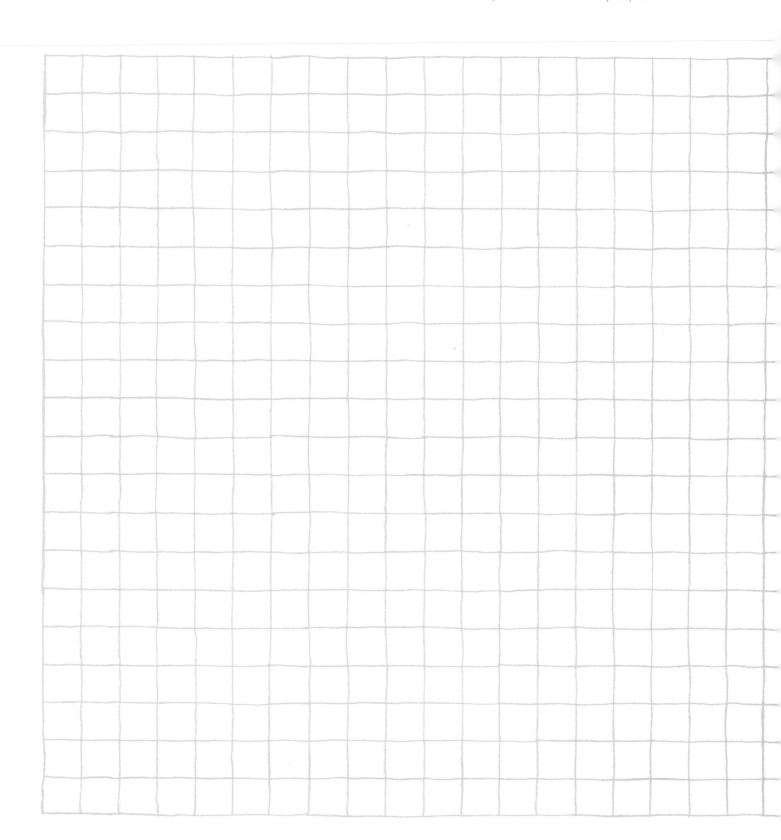

London: 13 million

Tokyo: 13 million

Mumbai: 18 million

Paris: 2 million

New York: 8 million

Beijing: 20 million

Sydney: 4 million

Rio: 6 million

Lagos: 21 million

Depicting the World

In ancient times, the world was thought to be a flat disk. This picture shows a traveller who has reached the end of the world and is poking his head through to the chaos beyond.

Now we know the earth is round –
but this is a problem for mapping.
How can we translate a sphere
onto a flat surface?

Map of the World

Mark the seven continents
on this map. Which countries
do you recognise?

All maps of the world are
known as 'projection maps'.
Using various mathematical
formulas, the world is ironed
out to fit on a flat page.
But in order for that to
happen, some parts
of the map have to be
stretched or compressed.

Where are you?
Colour your country in red.

Asia

Land area:	44,579,000 km² (the biggest!)
Population:	4.43 billion (the most populous!)
Number of countries:	48 (Russia and Turkey straddle Europe and Asia)
Biggest country:	China, 9,596,961 km²
Smallest country:	Maldives, 300 km²
Richest country:	China
Poorest country:	Tuvalu
Longest life expectancy:	Japan, 84
Shortest life expectancy:	Afghanistan, 52
Languages:	40 recognised languages
Most populous city:	Tokyo, 13,400,000
Highest peak:	Mount Everest, Nepal/China, 8,848 m
Longest river:	Yangtze, China, 6,300 km
Most polluted city:	New Delhi, India
Most polluting country:	China
Most endangered species:	Snow leopard

Can you find the countries on the map?

The Gobi Desert in Mongolia and China covers 1,295,000 km². It is a cold desert. The Himalayas create a 'rain shadow', blocking rain-carrying clouds from reaching the area.

RUSSIA

KAZAKHSTAN

GEORGIA
ARMENIA AZERBAIJAN
UZBEKISTAN
TURKMENISTAN
TURKEY
TA
LEBANON SYRIA
IRAQ
IRAN
AFGHANISTAN
ISRAEL
JORDAN
PAKISTAN
KUWAIT
QATAR
UAE
SAUDI ARABIA
OMAN
YEMEN

More people speak Mandarin than any other language in the world.

33% China has a population of 1.4 billion, and India has a population of 1.3 billion. Together they make up 1/3 of the world's population!

828 m The height of the tallest building in the world, the Burj Khalifa, in Dubai.

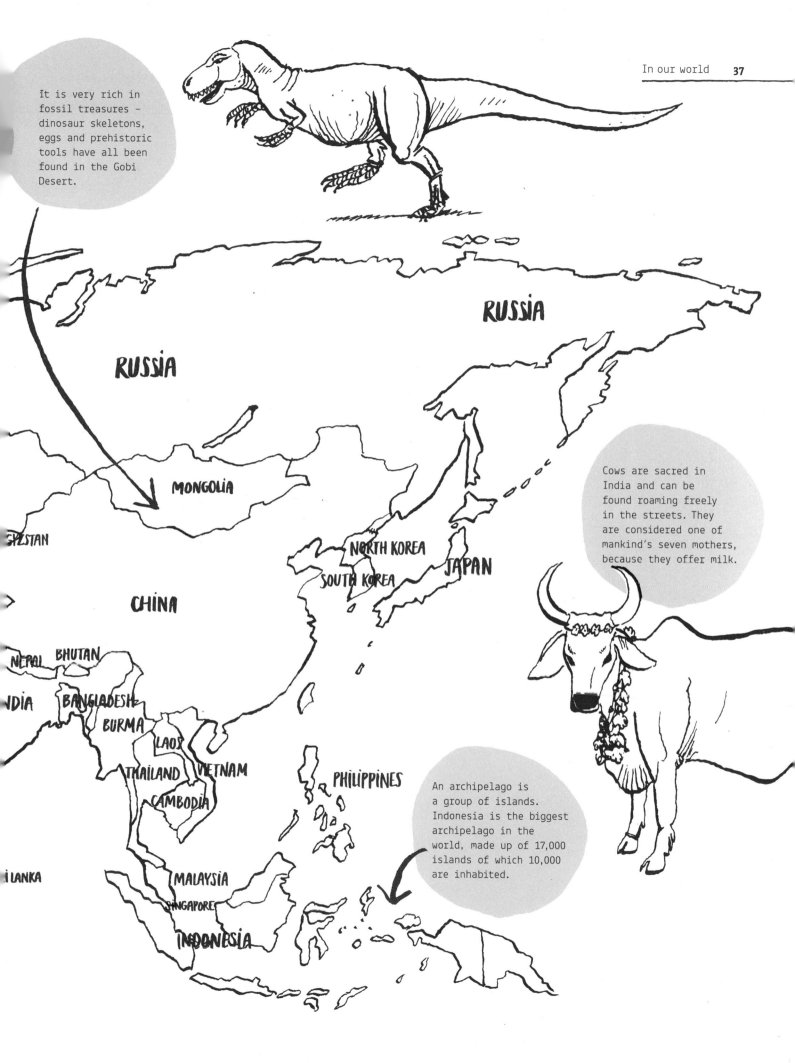

It is very rich in fossil treasures – dinosaur skeletons, eggs and prehistoric tools have all been found in the Gobi Desert.

RUSSIA

RUSSIA

MONGOLIA

GYZSTAN

NORTH KOREA

SOUTH KOREA

JAPAN

Cows are sacred in India and can be found roaming freely in the streets. They are considered one of mankind's seven mothers, because they offer milk.

CHINA

NEPAL   BHUTAN

NDIA

BANGLADESH

BURMA

LAOS

THAILAND   VIETNAM

CAMBODIA

PHILIPPINES

An archipelago is a group of islands. Indonesia is the biggest archipelago in the world, made up of 17,000 islands of which 10,000 are inhabited.

I LANKA

MALAYSIA

SINGAPORE

INDONESIA

Europe

Land area:	9,900,000 km²
Population:	740 million
Number of countries:	46 (Russia and Turkey straddle Europe and Asia)
Countries in the European Union:	27
Biggest country:	Russia, 17,098,242 km²
Smallest country:	Vatican City, 44 hectares
Richest country:	Germany
Poorest country:	Moldova
Most populous city:	Istanbul, 14,377,018
Longest life expectancy:	Iceland, 83.3
Shortest life expectancy:	Ukraine, 69
Languages:	23 official languages
Most polluted city:	Pernik, Bulgaria
Most polluting country:	Germany
Tallest building:	Federation Tower, Moscow, 373 m (London's Shard is only 308 m)
Longest river:	The Volga, Russia, 3,688 km
Highest peak:	Mont Blanc, France, 4,810 m
Most endangered animal:	Iberian lynx

ICELAND

IRELAND

UNITED KINGDOM

FRANCE

PORTUGAL

SPAIN

10.1% of world exports come from Germany. Germany is the largest exporter of goods in Europe.

There are over 1,000 different types of cheese made in France and over 140 different types of pasta made in Italy.

Denmark is considered the least corrupt country in the world.

Dutch people are the tallest in the world, with an average height of 185 cm for men and 170 cm for women.

25% of Russia is covered by trees.

NORWAY

FINLAND

SWEDEN

ESTONIA

LATVIA

LITHUANIA

DENMARK

RUSSIA

BELARUS

NETHERLANDS

GERMANY

POLAND

iUM

LUXEMBOURG

CZECH REPUBLIC

UKRAINE

SLOVAKIA

MOLDOVA

SWITZERLAND

AUSTRIA

HUNGARY

SLOVENIA

ROMANIA

GEORGIA

CROATIA

MONACO

ITALY

BOSNIA& HERZEGOVINA

SERBIA

BULGARIA

MONTENEGRO

KOSOVO

MACEDONIA

ALBANIA

TURKEY

GREECE

CYPRUS

Africa

Land area:	30,221,532 km²
Population:	1.1 billion
Number of countries:	54
Biggest country:	Algeria, 2,381,741 km²
Smallest country:	Gambia, 11,300 km²
Richest country:	Nigeria
Poorest country:	Congo
Longest life expectancy:	Morocco, 76
Shortest life expectancy:	Chad, 45
Languages:	There are 24 official languages spoken in Africa but over 2.000 other native languages in use
Most populous city:	Lagos, Nigeria, 21,000,000
Highest peak:	Mount Kilimanjaro, Tanzania, 5,895 m
Largest lake:	Lake Victoria, Kenya/Uganda/Tanzania, 68,800 km²
Tallest building:	Carlton Centre, South Africa, 223 m
Most endangered animal:	Addax

The world's tallest mammal is the giraffe.

Can you find the countries on the map?

38% of African adults are illiterate of which 2/3 are women.

30%

Although it is the poorest and least developed continent, Africa is very rich in minerals – it has 30% of the world's mineral resources including 40% of gold and 90% of platinum.

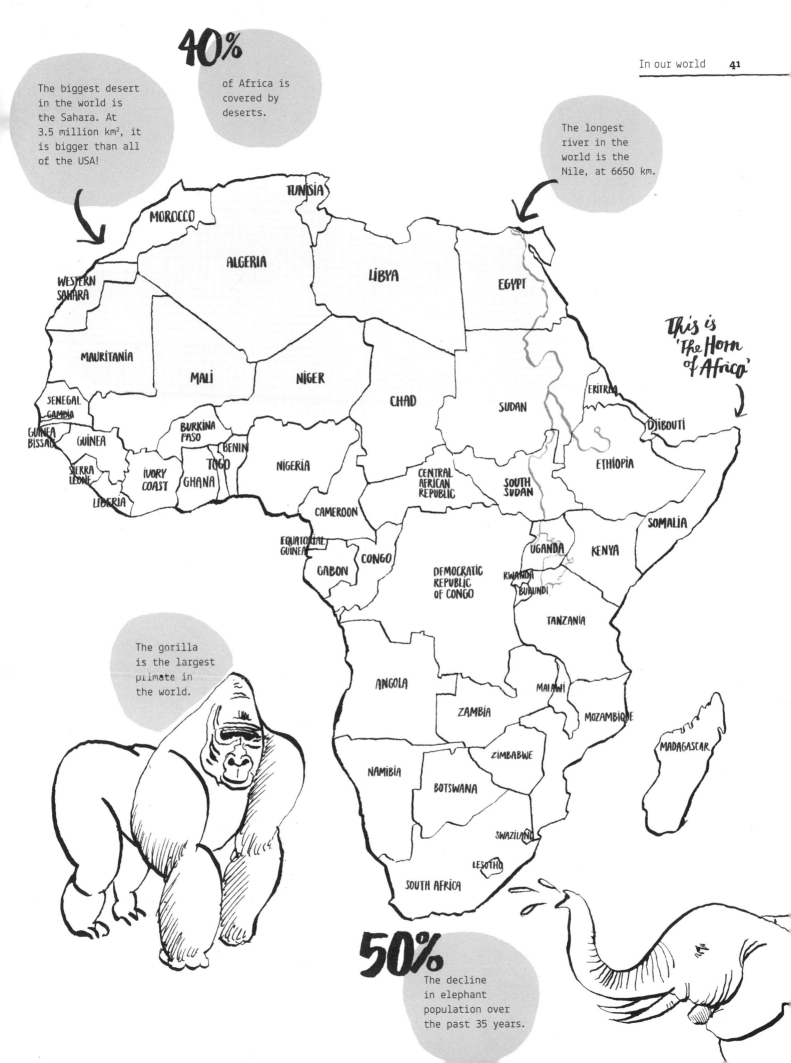

40%

The biggest desert in the world is the Sahara. At 3.5 million km², it is bigger than all of the USA!

of Africa is covered by deserts.

The longest river in the world is the Nile, at 6650 km.

This is 'The Horn of Africa'

The gorilla is the largest primate in the world.

50%

The decline in elephant population over the past 35 years.

North America

4.3% The USA makes up **4.3%** of the world's population and consumes **22%** of the world's oil.

Land area:	24,238,000 km^2
Population:	560 million
Number of countries:	23
Biggest country:	Canada, 9,976,140 km^2
Smallest country:	St Kitts and Nevis, 261 km^2
Richest country:	USA
Poorest country:	El Salvador
Longest life expectancy:	Canada, 81.9
Shortest life expectancy:	Haiti, 62.8
Languages:	16 recognised languages
Most populous city:	Mexico City, 21,000,000
Highest peak:	Mount McKinley, Alaska, 6,194 m
Lowest point:	Death Valley, California, 89 m below sea level
Largest lake:	Lake Superior, Canada, 83,270 km^2
Longest river:	Mississippi-Missouri, 6,019 km
Tallest building:	One World Trade Centre, New York, 541 m
Most endangered animal:	Red wolf

The largest living organism in the world is a honey fungus found in Oregon, measuring 8.9 km^2. It is estimated to be 2,400 years old.

HAWAII (USA)

Hawaii is the most isolated population center on Earth. Hawaii is 3,846 km from the coast of California and 6,196 km from Japan.

The Panama Canal is the only waterway to connect the Atlantic and Pacific oceans.

Canada has the longest coastline of any country in the world at

243,977 km

The highest tides in the world happen in the Bay of Fundy in New Brunswick, Canada.

ALASKA (USA)

The USA's richest states are Washington DC, New Jersey and Connecticut. The poorest states are Mississippi, West Virginia and Alabama.

CANADA

2000 km

The length of Yonge Street, which runs from Ontario to Minnesota - the longest street in the world!

UNITED STATES OF AMERICA

Yonge St

MEXICO

Central America is an isthmus, or land-bridge, that connects North and South America, with the Atlantic and Pacific oceans on either side.

There is no spot in Central America further than 200 km from the ocean.

BAHAMAS

CUBA

TURKS & CAICOS

HAITI

PUERTO RICO

JAMAICA

DOMINICAN REPUBLIC

GUATEMALA   BELIZE

HONDURAS

EL SALVADOR   NICARAGUA

PANAMA

COSTA RICA

South America

Land area:	17,840,000 km²
Population:	387.5 million
Number of countries:	12
Biggest country:	Brazil, 17,840,000 km²
Smallest country:	Suriname, 161,470 km²
Richest country:	Brazil
Poorest country:	Guyana
Longest life expectancy:	Chile, 80
Shortest life expectancy:	Guyana, 63
Languages:	Most people in South America speak Spanish or Portuguese, but there are more than 500 other languages spoken by indigenous peoples
Most populous city:	Sao Paolo, Brazil, 10,886,518
Highest peak:	Cerro Aconcagua, Argentina, 6,959 m
Largest lake:	Lake Titicaca, Bolivia/Peru, 8,340 km²
Longest river:	Amazon, Brazil, 6,439 km
Most polluted city:	Lima, Peru
Most endangered species:	Black-faced lion tamarind

Can you find the countries on the map?

3.5 million

slaves were brought from Africa to Brazil in the 16th to 19th Centuries.

40%

of the world's plant and animal species are found in the Amazon Rainforest.

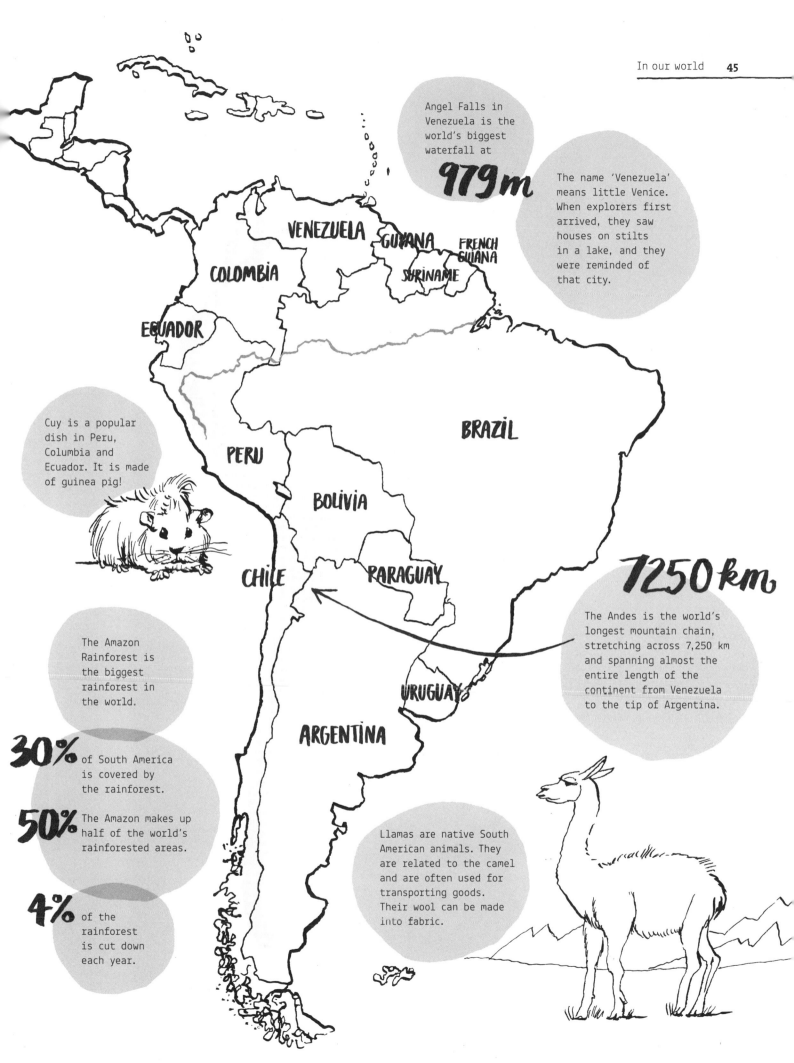

Angel Falls in Venezuela is the world's biggest waterfall at

979m

The name 'Venezuela' means little Venice. When explorers first arrived, they saw houses on stilts in a lake, and they were reminded of that city.

VENEZUELA

GUYANA

FRENCH GUIANA

COLOMBIA

SURINAME

ECUADOR

Cuy is a popular dish in Peru, Columbia and Ecuador. It is made of guinea pig!

BRAZIL

PERU

BOLIVIA

7250km

The Andes is the world's longest mountain chain, stretching across 7,250 km and spanning almost the entire length of the continent from Venezuela to the tip of Argentina.

CHILE

PARAGUAY

The Amazon Rainforest is the biggest rainforest in the world.

URUGUAY

30% of South America is covered by the rainforest.

ARGENTINA

50% The Amazon makes up half of the world's rainforested areas.

Llamas are native South American animals. They are related to the camel and are often used for transporting goods. Their wool can be made into fabric.

4% of the rainforest is cut down each year.

Australia and Oceania

The "continent" of Australia/Oceania includes the landmass of Australia and over 25,000 islands scattered across the Pacific Ocean, many of which are uninhabited.

Land area:	8,600,000 km²
Population:	36,000,000
Countries:	14
Biggest country:	Australia 7,686,850 km²
Smallest country:	Nauru, 21 km²
Richest country:	Australia
Poorest country:	Papua New Guinea
Longest life expectancy:	Australia, 82.3
Shortest life expectancy:	Marshall Islands, 59.5

Most of the native mammals of Australia are marsupials – that means that their babies develop inside a pouch instead of inside their bodies.

FEDERATED STATES OF MICRONESIA

MARSHALL ISLANDS

KIRIBATI

SOLOMON ISLANDS

SANTA CRUZ ISLANDS

TUVALU

PAPUA NEW GUINEA

VANUATU

NEW CALEDONIA

AUSTRALIA

As a giant island, Australia's wildlife is very unique. 83% of mammals and 89% of Australian reptiles don't exist anywhere else on earth.

NEW ZEALAND

Languages:	English is spoken in Australia and English and French are the recognised languages of most of the other countries, but there are over 1,000 indigenous languages spoken
Most populous city:	Sydney, Australia, 4,667,283
Highest mountain:	Mt Kosciuszko, Australia, 2228 m
Biggest rock:	Uluru (or Ayers Rock), Australia, 863 m
Longest River:	Murray-Darling, Australia, 3750 km
Most endangered species:	Mountain pygmy possum

Eucalyptus oil is highly flammable, which is why there are so many bush fires in Australia.

The longest place name in the world is a hill in New Zealand called Taumatawhakatangi-hangakoauauotamateapo-kaiwhenuakitanatahu.

COOK ISLANDS

FRENCH POLYNESIA

PITCAIRN ISLANDS

The Great Barrier Reef is the biggest coral reef in the world, covering over 2,000 km². It is home to 1,500 species of fish and 4,000 species of molluscs. It is very vulnerable to the effects of pollution and climate change, and since 1985, the Great Barrier Reef has lost more than half of its corals.

The Kiwi is the national bird of New Zealand, and 'Kiwi' is also internationally used as a nickname for people from New Zealand.

Antarctica

Land area:	14,000,000 km² (almost double the size of Australia)
Population:	1,000 in winter, 5,000 in summer
Country:	1
Coldest recorded temperature:	-89.2° C
Highest peak:	Vinson Massif 4,892 m
Most endangered animal:	Blue whale

LARSEN ICE SHELF

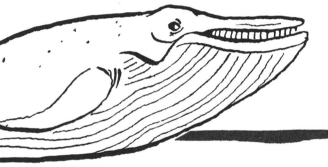

98% of Antarctica is covered by a huge ice sheet.

70% of the world's fresh water is contained in this ice sheet.

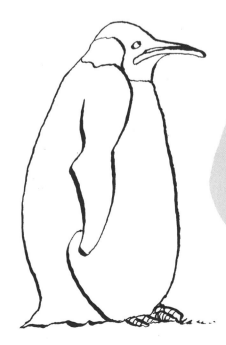

Antarctica is much colder than the Arctic. The only warm-blooded animal to stay on the continent throughout the bitter winter is the emperor penguin. There are no land mammals that live on Antarctica.

1895

The year the first human set foot on Antarctica.

60m

The level the oceans of the world would rise by if the ice in Antarctica were to melt.

AMERY ICE SHELF

NNE ICE SHELF

EAST ANTARCTICA

SOUTH POLE

WEST ANTARCTICA

GEOMAGNETIC
SOUTH POLE

ROSS ICE SHELF

The area below 60 degrees south enjoys one long day and one long night each year. The sun sets in March and rises in October.

At the beginning of winter, the Antarctic sea ice begins to expand, advancing around 100,000 km² per day, eventually doubling the size of Antarctica. In the summer this melts and disperses.

My Country

Draw a map of the country you live in. Mark the major cities, rivers, mountains and lakes. What interesting facts do you know about your country?

KEY

Imaginary Lines

On a world map there are some imaginary lines that help us identify where we are. These are called lines of latitude and longitude.

The Tropic of Cancer is at 23.5° north of the Equator and The Tropic of Capricorn is at 23.6° south of the Equator.

Countries between these two imaginary lines are close to the Equator and have warm temperatures all through the year.

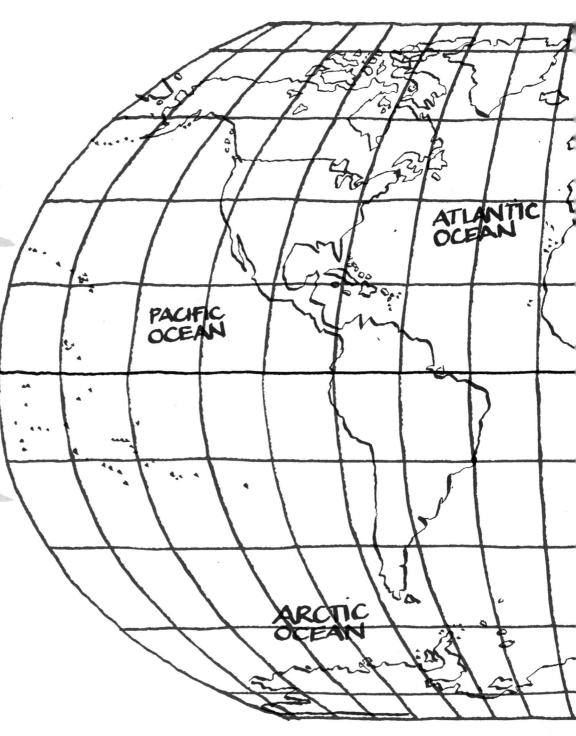

ATLANTIC OCEAN

PACIFIC OCEAN

ARCTIC OCEAN

-160° -120° -80° -40° W

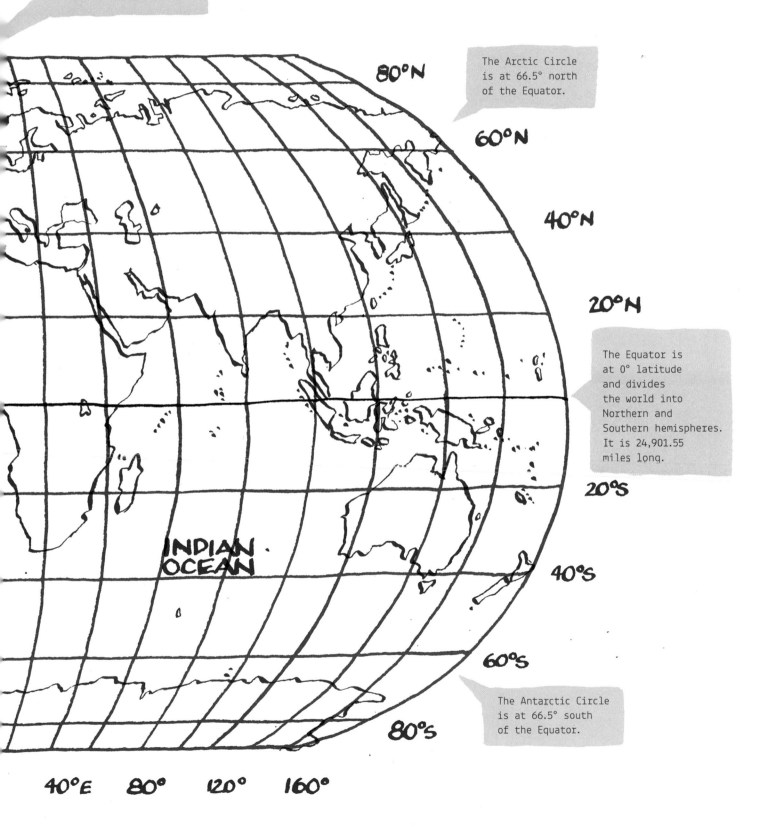

The Prime Meridian is at 0° longitude and divides the Earth into Eastern and Western hemispheres.

The Arctic Circle is at 66.5° north of the Equator.

The Equator is at 0° latitude and divides the world into Northern and Southern hemispheres. It is 24,901.55 miles long.

The Antarctic Circle is at 66.5° south of the Equator.

Tick the countries you have visited.
Circle the ones you would most like
to visit.

- ☐ **Afghanistan** *Asia*
- ☐ **Albania** *Europe*
- ☐ **Algeria** *Africa*
- ☐ **American Samoa** *Australasia*
- ☐ **Andorra** *Europe*
- ☐ **Angola** *Africa*
- ☐ **Anguilla** *Caribbean*
- ☐ **Antigua & Barbuda** *Caribbean*
- ☐ **Argentina** *South America*
- ☐ **Armenia** *Europe*
- ☐ **Aruba** *Caribbean*
- ☐ **Australia** *Australasia*
- ☐ **Austria** *Europe*
- ☐ **Azerbaijan** *Europe*
- ☐ **Bahamas** *Caribbean*
- ☐ **Bahrain** *Middle East*
- ☐ **Bangladesh** *Asia*
- ☐ **Barbados** *Caribbean*
- ☐ **Belarus** *Europe*
- ☐ **Belgium** *Europe*
- ☐ **Belize** *North America*
- ☐ **Benin** *Africa*
- ☐ **Bermuda** *Caribbean*
- ☐ **Bhutan** *Asia*
- ☐ **Bolivia** *South America*
- ☐ **Bosnia-Herzegovina** *Europe*
- ☐ **Botswana** *Africa*
- ☐ **Bouvet** Island *Africa*
- ☐ **Brazil** *South America*
- ☐ **Brunei** *Asia*
- ☐ **Bulgaria** *Europe*
- ☐ **Burkina Faso** *Africa*
- ☐ **Burundi** *Africa*
- ☐ **Cambodia** *Asia*
- ☐ **Cameroon** *Africa*
- ☐ **Canada** *North America*
- ☐ **Cape Verde** *Africa*
- ☐ **Cayman Islands** *Caribbean*
- ☐ **Central African Republic** *Africa*
- ☐ **Chad** *Africa*

- ☐ **Chile** *South America*
- ☐ **China** *Asia*
- ☐ **Christmas Island** *Australasia*
- ☐ **Cocos (Keeling) Islands** *Australasia*
- ☐ **Colombia** *South America*
- ☐ **Comoros** *Africa*
- ☐ **Congo, Democratic Republic of the (Zaire)** *Africa*
- ☐ **Congo, Republic of** *Africa*
- ☐ **Cook Islands** *Australasia*
- ☐ **Costa Rica** *North America*
- ☐ **Croatia** *Europe*
- ☐ **Cuba** *Caribbean*
- ☐ **Cyprus** *Europe*
- ☐ **Czech Republic** *Europe*
- ☐ **Denmark** *Europe*
- ☐ **Djibouti** *Africa*
- ☐ **Dominica** *Caribbean*
- ☐ **Dominican Republic** *Caribbean*
- ☐ **Ecuador** *South America*
- ☐ **Egypt** *Africa*
- ☐ **El Salvador** *North America*
- ☐ **Equatorial Guinea** *Africa*
- ☐ **Eritrea** *Africa*
- ☐ **Estonia** *Europe*
- ☐ **Ethiopia** *Africa*
- ☐ **Falkland Islands** *South America*
- ☐ **Faroe Islands** *Europe*
- ☐ **Fiji** *Australasia*
- ☐ **Finland** *Europe*
- ☐ **France** *Europe*
- ☐ **French Guiana** *South America*
- ☐ **Gabon** *Africa*
- ☐ **Gambia** *Africa*
- ☐ **Georgia** *Europe*
- ☐ **Germany** *Europe*
- ☐ **Ghana** *Africa*
- ☐ **Gibraltar** *Europe*
- ☐ **Greece** *Europe*

- ☐ **Greenland** *Europe*
- ☐ **Grenada** *Caribbean*
- ☐ **Guadeloupe (French)** *Caribbean*
- ☐ **Guam (USA)** *Australasia*
- ☐ **Guatemala** *North America*
- ☐ **Guinea** *Africa*
- ☐ **Guinea Bissau** *Africa*
- ☐ **Guyana** *South America*
- ☐ **Haiti** *Caribbean*
- ☐ **Holy See** *Europe*
- ☐ **Honduras** *North America*
- ☐ **Hong Kong** *Asia*
- ☐ **Hungary** *Europe*
- ☐ **Iceland** *Europe*
- ☐ **India** *Asia*
- ☐ **Indonesia** *Asia*
- ☐ **Iran** *Middle East*
- ☐ **Iraq** *Middle East*
- ☐ **Ireland** *Europe*
- ☐ **Israel** *Middle East*
- ☐ **Italy** *Europe*
- ☐ **Ivory Coast (Cote D'Ivoire)** *Africa*
- ☐ **Jamaica** *Caribbean*
- ☐ **Japan** *Asia*
- ☐ **Jordan** *Middle East*
- ☐ **Kazakhstan** *Asia*
- ☐ **Kenya** *Africa*
- ☐ **Kiribati** *Australasia*
- ☐ **Kuwait** *Middle East*
- ☐ **Kyrgyzstan** *Asia*
- ☐ **Laos** *Asia*
- ☐ **Latvia** *Europe*
- ☐ **Lebanon** *Middle East*
- ☐ **Lesotho** *Africa*
- ☐ **Liberia** *Africa*
- ☐ **Libya** *Africa*
- ☐ **Liechtenstein** *Europe*
- ☐ **Lithuania** *Europe*
- ☐ **Luxembourg** *Europe*
- ☐ **Macau** *Asia*

- [ ] Macedonia *Europe*
- [ ] Madagascar *Africa*
- [ ] Malawi *Africa*
- [ ] Malaysia *Asia*
- [ ] Maldives *Asia*
- [ ] Mali *Africa*
- [ ] Malta *Europe*
- [ ] Marshall Islands *Australasia*
- [ ] Martinique (French) *Caribbean*
- [ ] Mauritania *Africa*
- [ ] Mauritius *Africa*
- [ ] Mayotte *Africa*
- [ ] Mexico *North America*
- [ ] Micronesia *Australasia*
- [ ] Moldova *Europe*
- [ ] Monaco *Europe*
- [ ] Mongolia *Asia*
- [ ] Montenegro *Europe*
- [ ] Montserrat *Caribbean*
- [ ] Morocco *Africa*
- [ ] Mozambique *Africa*
- [ ] Myanmar *Asia*
- [ ] Namibia *Africa*
- [ ] Nauru *Australasia*
- [ ] Nepal *Asia*
- [ ] Netherlands *Europe*
- [ ] Netherlands Antilles *Caribbean*
- [ ] New Caledonia (French) *Australasia*
- [ ] New Zealand *Australasia*
- [ ] Nicaragua *North America*
- [ ] Niger *Africa*
- [ ] Nigeria *Africa*
- [ ] Niue *Australasia*
- [ ] Norfolk Island *Australasia*
- [ ] North Korea *Asia*
- [ ] Northern Mariana Islands *Asia*
- [ ] Norway *Europe*
- [ ] Oman *Middle East*
- [ ] Pakistan *Asia*
- [ ] Palau *Australasia*

- [ ] Panama *North America*
- [ ] Papua New Guinea *Australasia*
- [ ] Paraguay *South America*
- [ ] Peru *South America*
- [ ] Philippines *Asia*
- [ ] Pitcairn Island *Australasia*
- [ ] Poland *Europe*
- [ ] Polynesia (French) *Australasia*
- [ ] Portugal *Europe*
- [ ] Puerto Rico *Caribbean*
- [ ] Qatar *Middle East*
- [ ] Reunion *Africa*
- [ ] Romania *Europe*
- [ ] Russia *Europe*
- [ ] Rwanda *Africa*
- [ ] Saint Helena *Africa*
- [ ] Saint Kitts and Nevis *Caribbean*
- [ ] Saint Lucia *Caribbean*
- [ ] Saint Pierre & Miquelon *North America*
- [ ] Saint Vincent & Grenadines *Caribbean*
- [ ] Samoa *Australasia*
- [ ] San Marino *Europe*
- [ ] Sao Tome & Principe *Africa*
- [ ] Saudi Arabia *Middle East*
- [ ] Senegal *Africa*
- [ ] Serbia *Europe*
- [ ] Seychelles *Africa*
- [ ] Sierra Leone *Africa*
- [ ] Singapore *Asia*
- [ ] Slovakia *Europe*
- [ ] Slovenia *Europe*
- [ ] Solomon Islands *Australasia*
- [ ] Somalia *Africa*
- [ ] South Africa *Africa*
- [ ] South Georgia & South Sandwich Islands *South America*
- [ ] South Korea *Asia*
- [ ] South Sudan *Africa*

- [ ] Spain *Europe*
- [ ] Sri Lanka *Asia*
- [ ] Sudan *Africa*
- [ ] Suriname *South America*
- [ ] Svalbard & Jan Mayen Islands *Europe*
- [ ] Swaziland *Africa*
- [ ] Sweden *Europe*
- [ ] Switzerland *Europe*
- [ ] Syria *Middle East*
- [ ] Tajikistan *Asia*
- [ ] Tanzania *Africa*
- [ ] Thailand *Asia*
- [ ] Timor-Leste (East Timor) *Australasia*
- [ ] Togo *Africa*
- [ ] Tokelau *Australasia*
- [ ] Tonga *Australasia*
- [ ] Trinidad & Tobago *Caribbean*
- [ ] Tunisia *Africa*
- [ ] Turkey *Middle East*
- [ ] Turkmenistan *Asia*
- [ ] Turks & Caicos Islands *Caribbean*
- [ ] Tuvalu *Australasia*
- [ ] Uganda *Africa*
- [ ] Ukraine *Europe*
- [ ] United Arab Emirates *Middle East*
- [ ] United Kingdom *Europe*
- [ ] United States *North America*
- [ ] Uruguay *South America*
- [ ] Uzbekistan *Asia*
- [ ] Vanuatu *Australasia*
- [ ] Venezuela *South America*
- [ ] Vietnam *Asia*
- [ ] Virgin Islands *Caribbean*
- [ ] Wallis & Futuna Islands *Australasia*
- [ ] Yemen *Middle East*
- [ ] Zambia *Africa*
- [ ] Zimbabwe *Africa*

Do you know which countries
these objects come from?

Japan!

Adaptations

Animals adapt to the habitats in which they live.

Polar bears and arctic foxes live in the Arctic. They have thick white fur to protect them from the cold and to camouflage with the snow.

Colour me in!

Penguins live in the Antarctic and have a thick layer of fat as well as insulating feathers to keep themselves warm. Emperor penguins huddle together against the bitter wind.

The wet, tropical climate of the rainforest allows many millions of species to thrive. Because there are so many animals competing for food, different species have evolved to eat specific things or to protect themselves from other animals that might want to eat them.

The sloth moves so slowly that algae grows on its fur, helping it to camouflage with the trees.

The spider monkey's tail is super strong, meaning it can use both its hands to pick and eat food.

The big beaks of toucans can crack nuts and snip the fruit off trees.

The tree frog is brightly coloured, warning predators to keep away - its skin is poisonous!

Dream country

Draw a map of an imaginary country. Mark its major cities, rivers, deserts, mountains and lakes.

KEY

Say Hello!

This is how you say 'hello' in different languages:

Bonjour! French

Bok! Croatian

Buon giorno! Italian

chum reap suor Cambodian

Guten Tag German

Dzień Dobry Polish

Hej Danish

Hoi Dutch

Swahili **Jambo**

¡Hola! Spanish

Konnichi ha Japanese

Names

These are some of the most
popular names in countries
around the world:

Country	Names
Egypt	MOHAMED & FATMA
Tunisia	MEHDI & MARIAM
Argentina	JUAN & SOFIA
Brazil	MIGUEL & SOPHIA
Haiti	STEVENSON & WIDELENE
Jamaica	JAYDEN & GABRIELLE
USA	NOAH & SOPHIA
Uruguay	AGUSTIN & FLORENCIA
India	AARAV & ANANYA
Israel	NOAM & NOA
Japan	HIROTO & YUINA
Philippines	JOHN PAUL & ALTHEA

Armenia	**DAVIT & NAREH**
Belarus	**MAXIM & MARIA**
Croatia	**LUKA & LANA**
France	**NATHAN & EMMA**
Germany	**BEN & MIA**
Greece	**GEORGIOS & MARIA**
Italy	**FRANCESCO & SOFIA**
Netherlands	**SEM & TESS**
Poland	**JACUB & LENA**
Russia	**ALEXANDER & ANASTASIA**
Spain	**HUGO & LUCIA**
Sweden	**LUCAS & ALICE**
UK	**OLIVER & AMELIA**

What is your name and what does it mean?

Housing

These are different types of houses from around the world. Colour them in and draw the families that live inside!

MUD HUT

In South Africa, the Ndebele people make round houses out of thick mud, with a thatched roof that stay cool in the summer.

JAPANESE HOUSE

In Japan, houses are traditionally made of wood with sloping roofs to keep off the heavy rain, and thin walls to keep the house cool in summer.

IGLOO

Inuit people in Canada build igloos out of blocks of snow, keeping the wind out and the warmth in.

YURT

In Mongolia people live in yurts that can be erected and taken down quite easily as herds move.

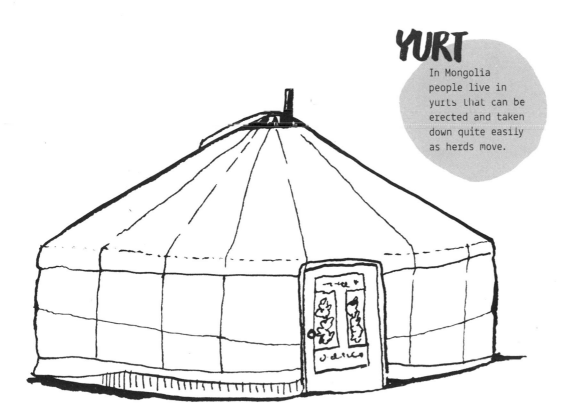

My House

Draw the house
of your dreams!

Money Money Money

These are some banknotes from around the world.

Now try designing
your own banknote!

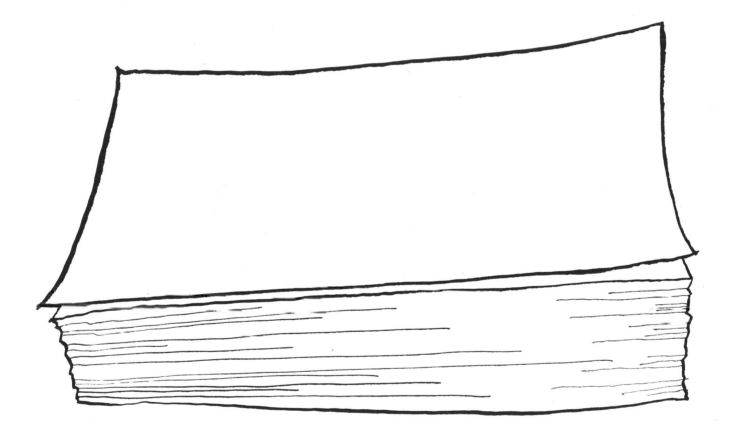

smallchange

Put some coins under this
page and colour over them
with a pencil or a crayon to
get a rubbing.

Flags

Different shapes and colours have different meanings on flags:

BLUE

Represents freedom, vigilance, peace, strength and patriotism.

GREEN

Symbolises the Earth, fertility, hope or the Muslim religion.

WHITE

Represents peace, innocence or snow. A simple white flag represents surrender.

RED

Represents bravery, revolution, hardiness and valour.

YELLOW

Represents generosity.

RED **GOLD** **GREEN**

Red, gold and green are the pan-African colours.

RED

The combination of Red, white and blue was used in the French Revolution and now represents independence and freedom.

WHITE **BLUE**

RED **WHITE**

Red, white, black and green are the pan-Arab colours.

BLACK **GREEN**

Flags are used to symbolise
nations and countries. Their
design often reflects aspects of
history, tradition or geography
that a nation takes pride in.

Have a look at the
South Korean flag:

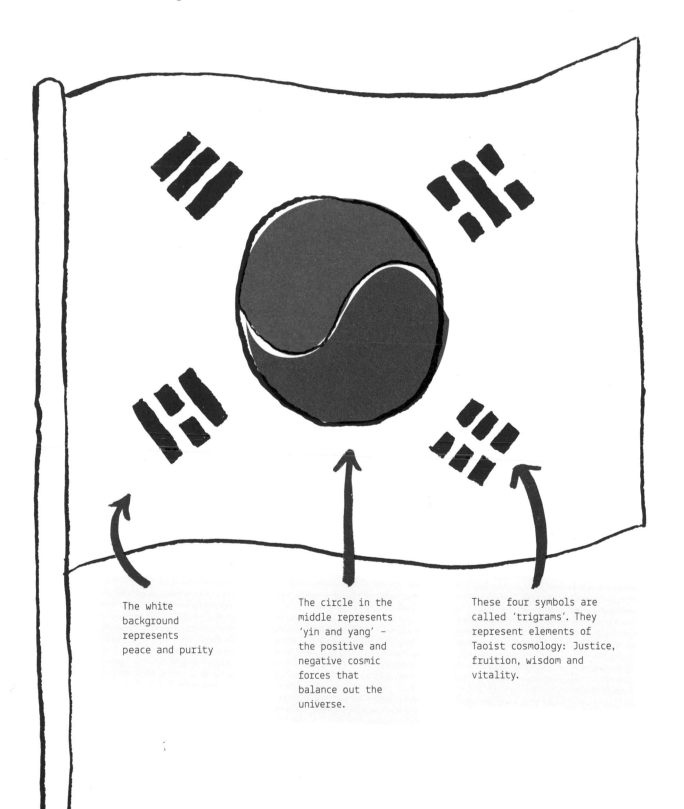

The white
background
represents
peace and purity

The circle in the
middle represents
'yin and yang' –
the positive and
negative cosmic
forces that
balance out the
universe.

These four symbols are
called 'trigrams'. They
represent elements of
Taoist cosmology: Justice,
fruition, wisdom and
vitality.

Flags

Do a little bit of research and
see if you can colour in these flags.

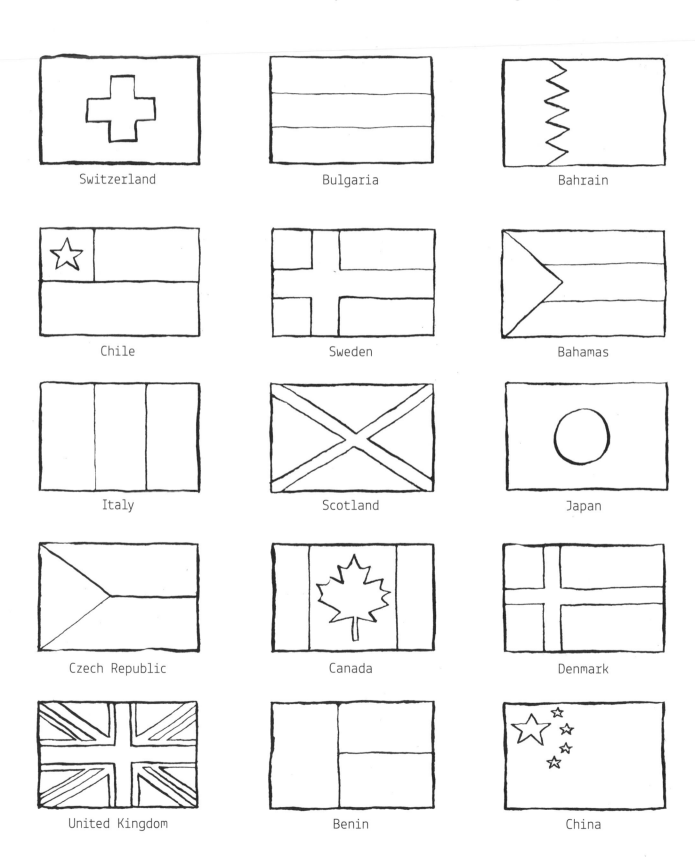

Switzerland

Bulgaria

Bahrain

Chile

Sweden

Bahamas

Italy

Scotland

Japan

Czech Republic

Canada

Denmark

United Kingdom

Benin

China

Argentina

Greenland

Antigua & Barbuda

United States

Ghana

South Korea

France

Turkey

South Africa

Cuba

Norway

Lebanon

Australia

Germany

Panama

Now design some flags for you and
your family! Make them symbolise
who you all are and where you come from.

Religions of the World

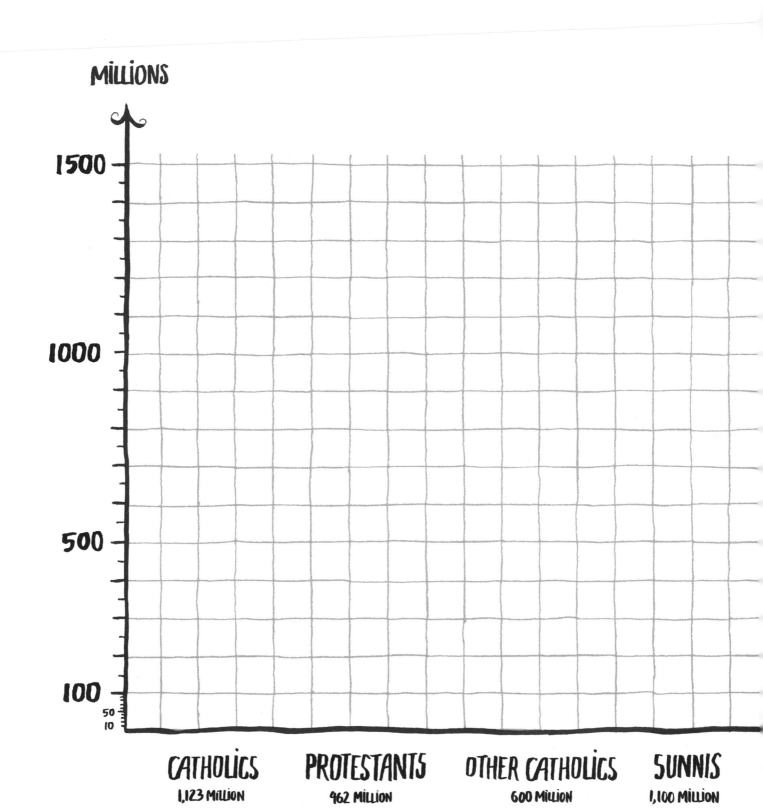

MILLIONS

1500

1000

500

100
50
10

CATHOLICS
1,123 Million

PROTESTANTS
462 Million

OTHER CATHOLICS
600 Million

SUNNIS
1,100 Million

Compare the numbers of
people that belong to the
world's main religions.

Fill in this bar graph,
colouring each religion
in a different colour.

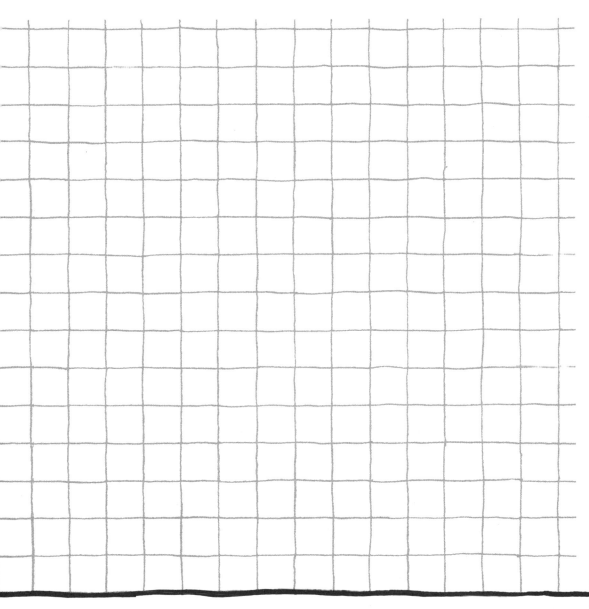

RELIGIONS

SHI'AS
192 MILLION

HINDUS
957 MILLION

BUDDHISTS
396 MILLION

SIKHS
23 MILLION

JEWS
13 MILLION

Traditions of the World

Even people of the same religion
have different traditions.
These are some Christmas dinners
from around the world.

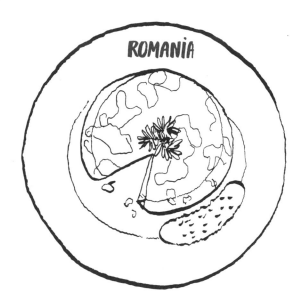

Beef in aspik

Goose or carp

Fried eel

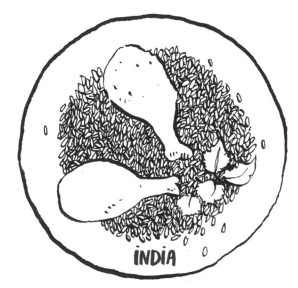

Chicken biryani

Lamb with vegetables

Smorgasbord

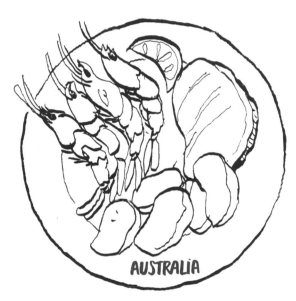

Prawn BBQ

Bacalao

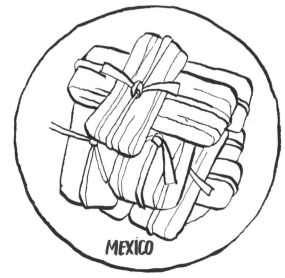

Tamales

Turkey with all the trimmings

Under the Sea

Oceans

Colour in the landlocked
countries - there aren't as many
of them as you might think!

Oceans make up 70% of our planet.
See how many you can identify
on this map.

OceanFacts

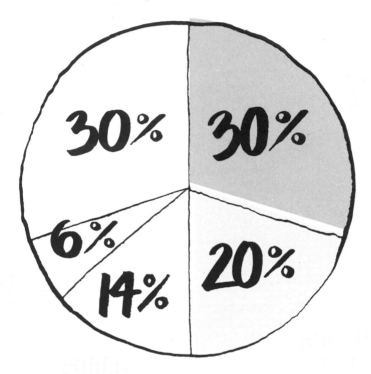

30% 30%

6% 14% 20%

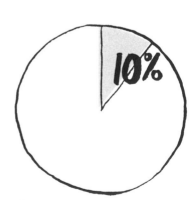

10%

of the earth's oceans
have been explored
by humans. Not much!

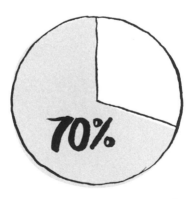

70%

of the oxygen
we breathe
is produced
by the oceans.

11,318t

The pressure at the deepest
point in the ocean is more
than 11,318 tons per m², or the
equivalent of one person trying
to support 50 jumbo jets.

As the world warms and the glaciers melt, sea levels are rising. The sea level has risen by 25 cm in the past 140 years.

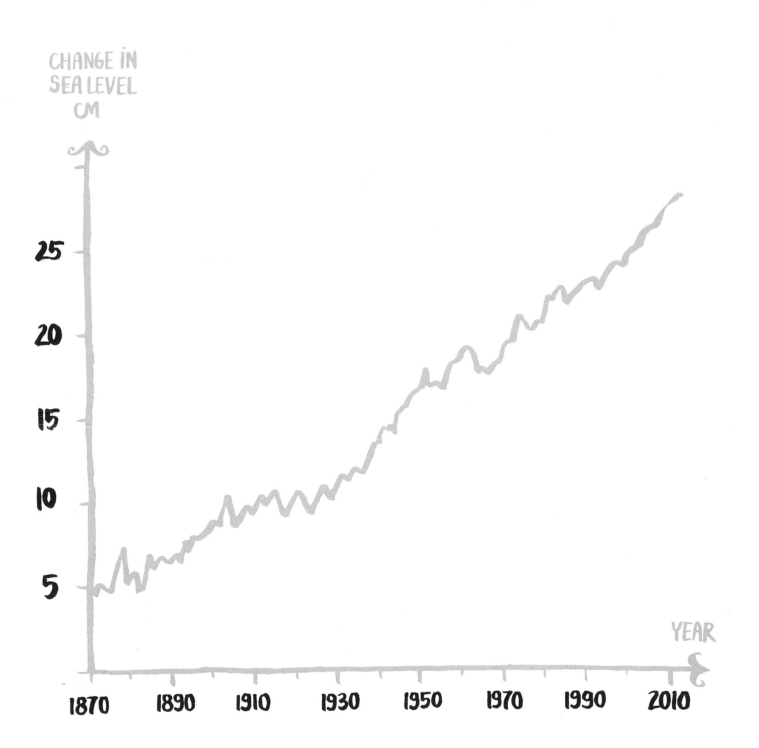

Glaciers

Glaciers are huge masses of compressed snow that have turned into ice over the course of hundreds of years.

Glaciers are constantly moving very, very slowly, under the force of their own weight. Occasionally they'll move much more quickly. This is called a 'surge'. The biggest surge ever documented was in 1953 – the Kutiah Glacier in Pakistan moved 12 km over a period of three months.

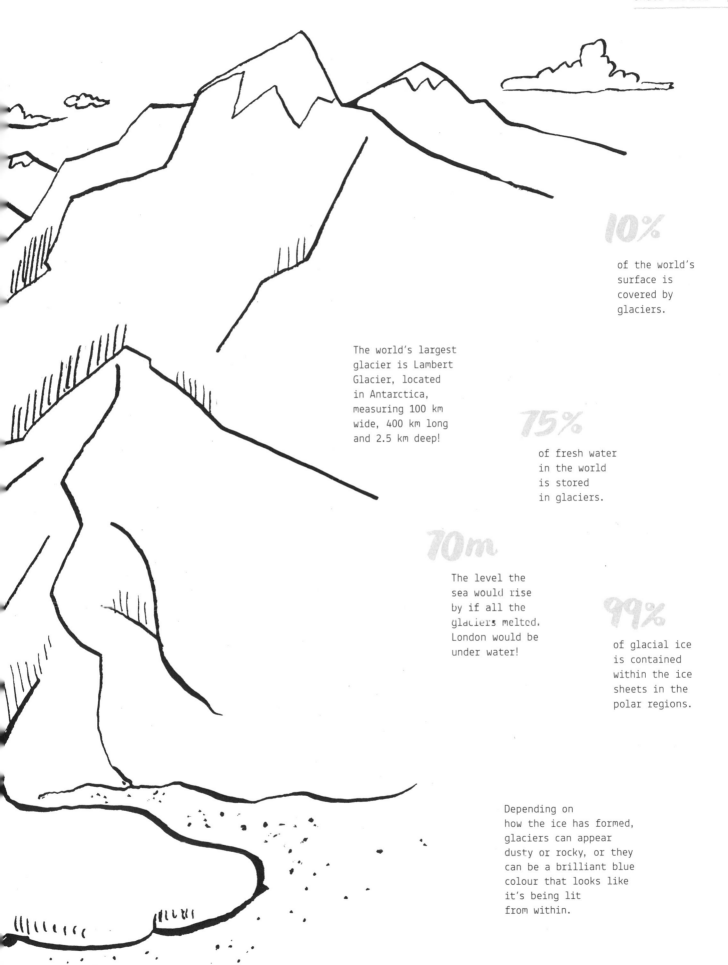

10% of the world's surface is covered by glaciers.

The world's largest glacier is Lambert Glacier, located in Antarctica, measuring 100 km wide, 400 km long and 2.5 km deep!

75% of fresh water in the world is stored in glaciers.

10m The level the sea would rise by if all the glaciers melted. London would be under water!

99% of glacial ice is contained within the ice sheets in the polar regions.

Depending on how the ice has formed, glaciers can appear dusty or rocky, or they can be a brilliant blue colour that looks like it's being lit from within.

Speedy Swimmers

These are the fastest
fish in the ocean.
Fill in the bar graph
and compare their speed!

SPEED
km/h

120
110
100
90
80
70
60
50
40
30
20
10

SAILFISH
112 km/h

STRIPED MARLIN
80 km/h

JACK MACKEREL
77 km/h

BLUE FIN TUNA
76 km/h

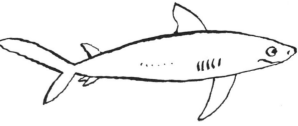

BLUE SHARK
69 km/h

Ocean Deep

Scientists
think that we
have discovered
less than half of
the animal species
that live in
the oceans.

The ocean trenches
reach depths of 11km
and are around 1° C
all year round. The
creatures who live
here are very strange.

The fangtooth fish lives
at depths of 5 km under
the ocean. It has such
big teeth that it has
evolved sockets on either
side of the brain to
accommodate its teeth
when its mouth is closed.

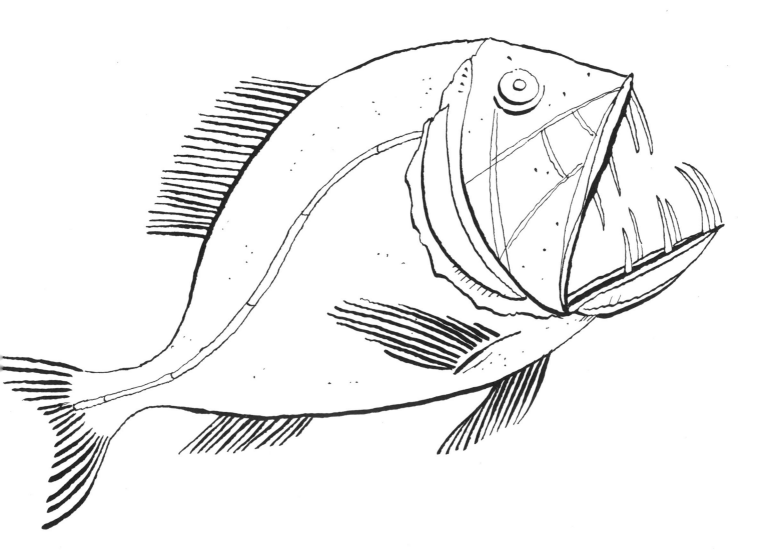

Draw a creature you think
might be hiding in the
deepest, darkest depths
of the ocean.

Deep Sea

SEA LEVEL

JOHN DORY

1,000 METERS

GURNARD

ANGLER FISH

4,000 METERS

BASSOGIGAS

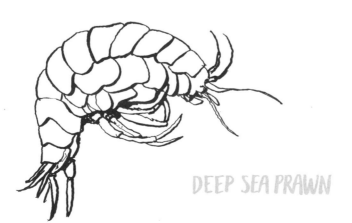

DEEP SEA PRAWN

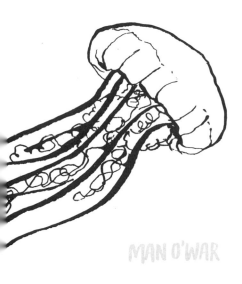

MAN O'WAR

COELACANTH

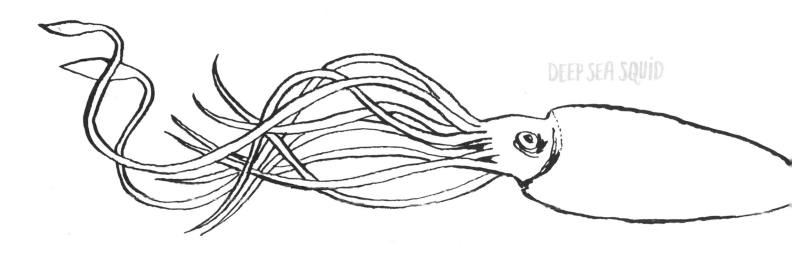

DEEP SEA SQUID

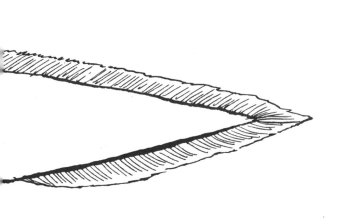

ETHUSA

plastic bag facts

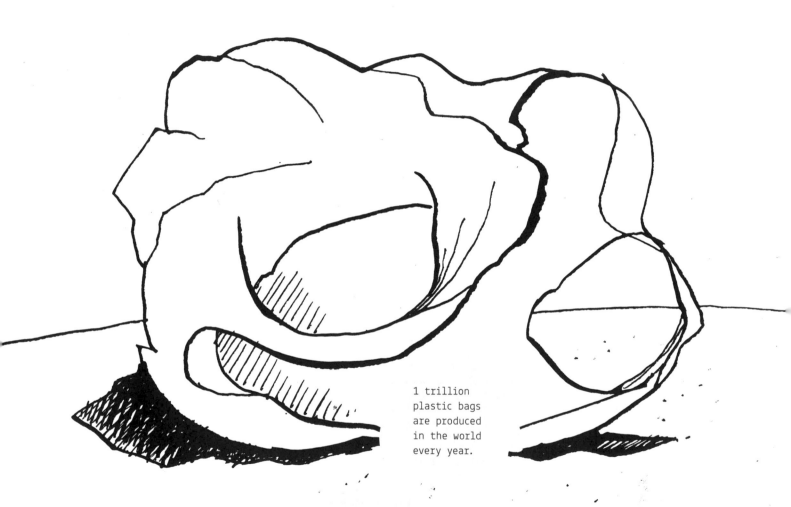

1 trillion
plastic bags
are produced
in the world
every year.

3.5 million tons
of plastic bags
are discarded
in a year.

It takes 1,000
years for one
plastic bag to
fully degrade.

In some parts
of the Pacific,
over 27,000
pieces of
plastic were
found in 1 km^2
of ocean.

The 'Pacific Garbage Patch' is an area in the Pacific Ocean where all the millions of tons of rubbish thrown away by humans converges. In some estimates, the area the garbage patch covers is almost twice the size of the USA!

1 square in the grid is 10 million km²

USA

PACIFIC GARBAGE PATCH

Overfishing

Overfishing is a major problem in ocean environments. Fish are being caught faster than they can reproduce. This has an impact on sea birds and other fish that feed on the fish that are being caught.

There has been an 83% decline in the population of bluefin tuna since 1950. Fill in the bar graph opposite to see why.

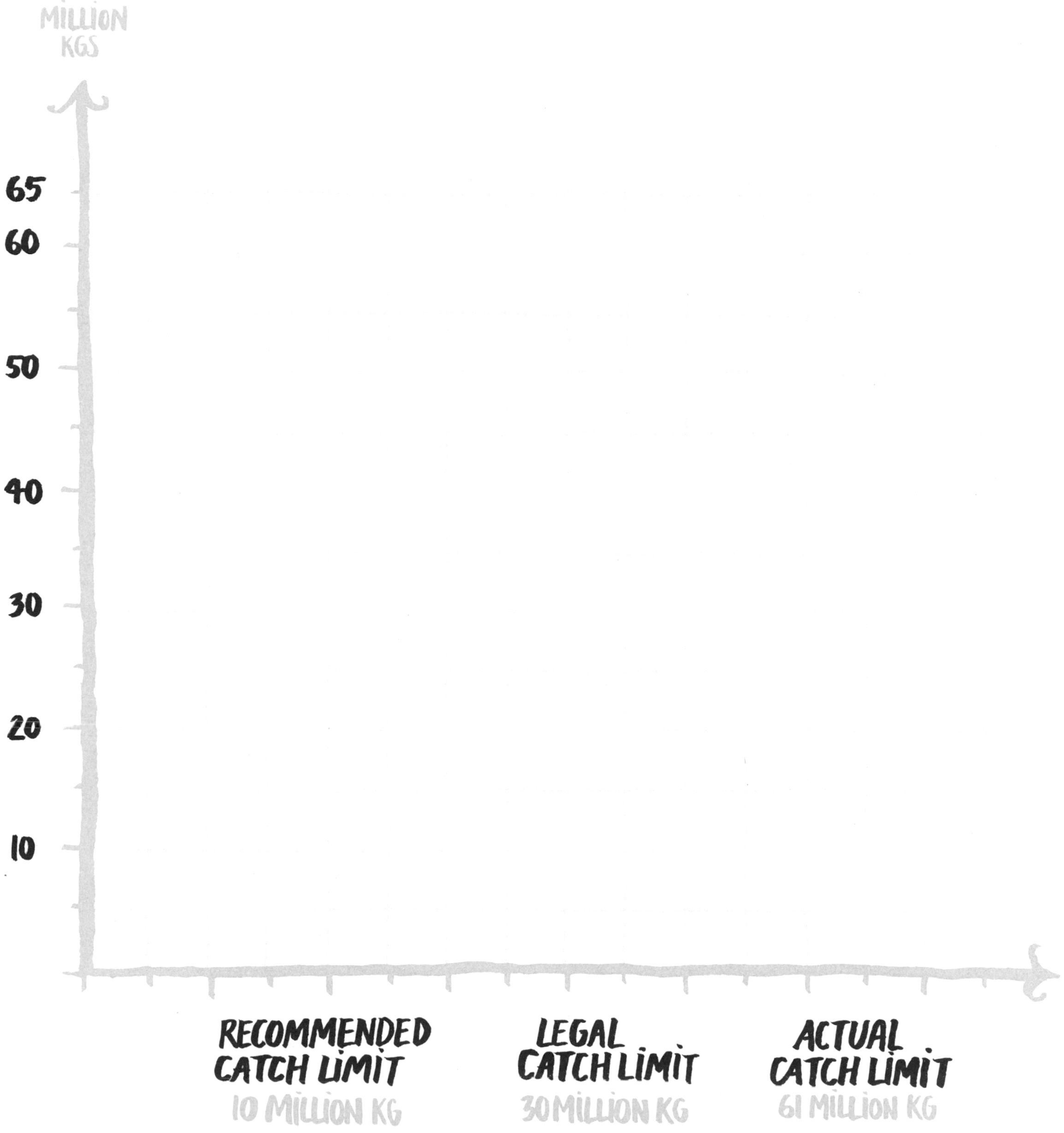

MILLION
KGS

65
60

50

40

30

20

10

RECOMMENDED
CATCH LIMIT
10 MILLION KG

LEGAL
CATCH LIMIT
30 MILLION KG

ACTUAL
CATCH LIMIT
61 MILLION KG

Tides

Sea-levels rise and fall due to the gravitational pull of the sun and the moon. These are called tides.

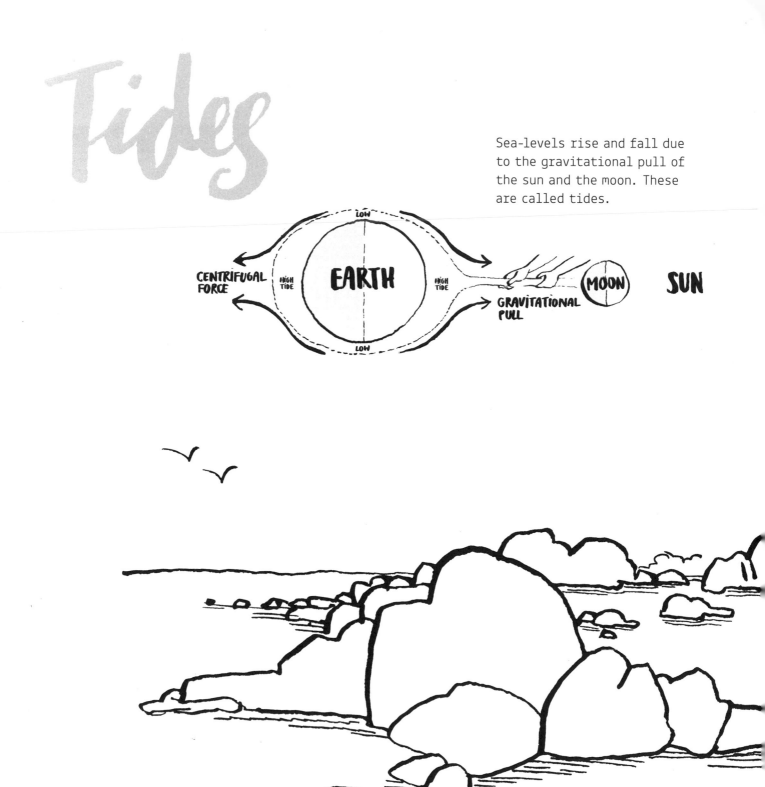

Tide pools are pools of sea water left in the rocky areas close to the ocean that are uncovered when the tide goes out.

Draw some things you might find in a tide pool.

Mussels   Crabs

Anemones   Winkles

Barnacles   Limpets

Lichen   Algae   Starfish

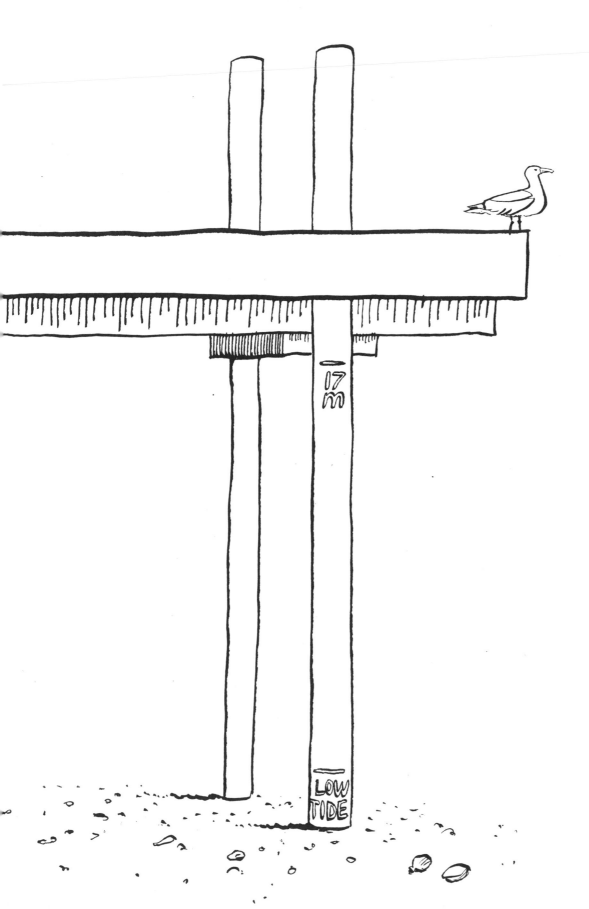

17
m

LOW
TIDE

The Bay of Fundy, in Canada,
has the biggest tidal range
in the world, rising by 16.3 m
at high tide.

Draw what you can see
at high and low tide.

Shipwreck

There are an estimated
3 million shipwrecks lying
on the seabeds.

The Mary Rose was a Tudor
warship that was sunk
by the French in 1545. She was
discovered and restored in 1982,
and gives us an amazing insight
into life and war in the days
of King Henry VIII.

colour. me in!

The skull and crossbones has been the pirate flag since the 18th Century. It's called the 'Jolly Roger' and it's thought that 'Roger' refers to an old nickname for the devil.

Draw a treasure map!

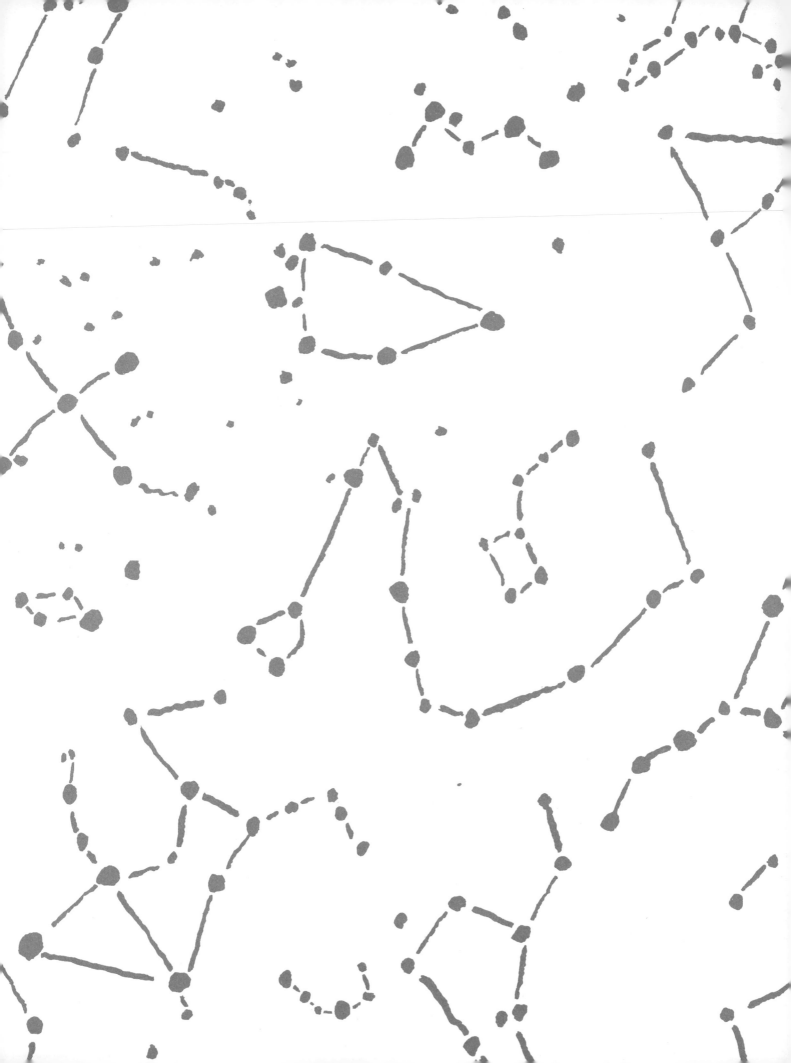

Out of our World

Planets

Can you name all the planets
in our solar system?

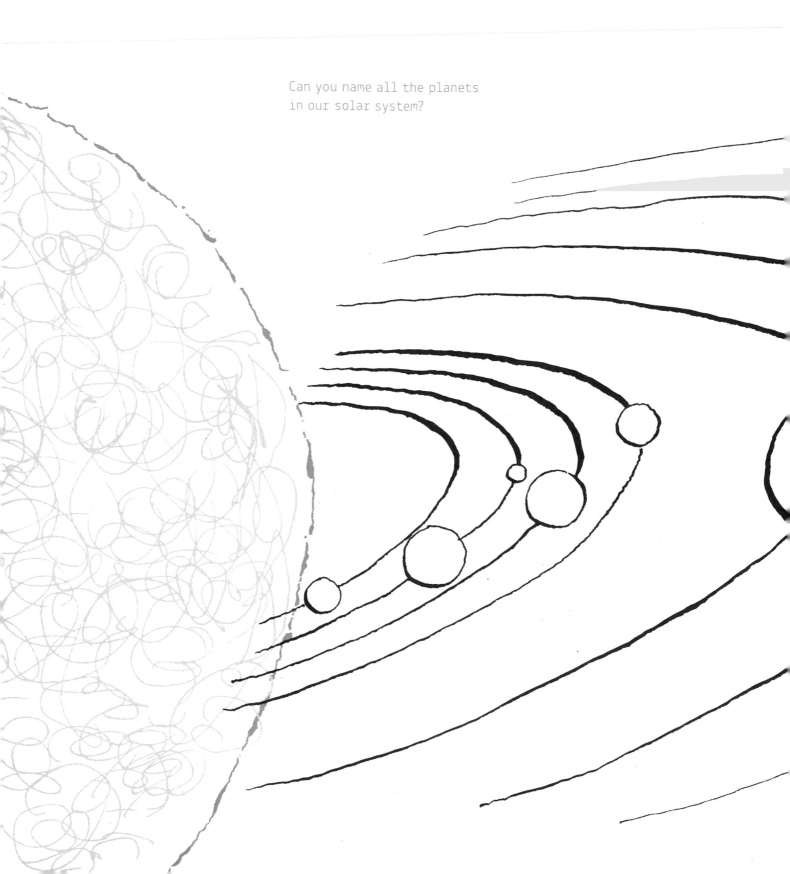

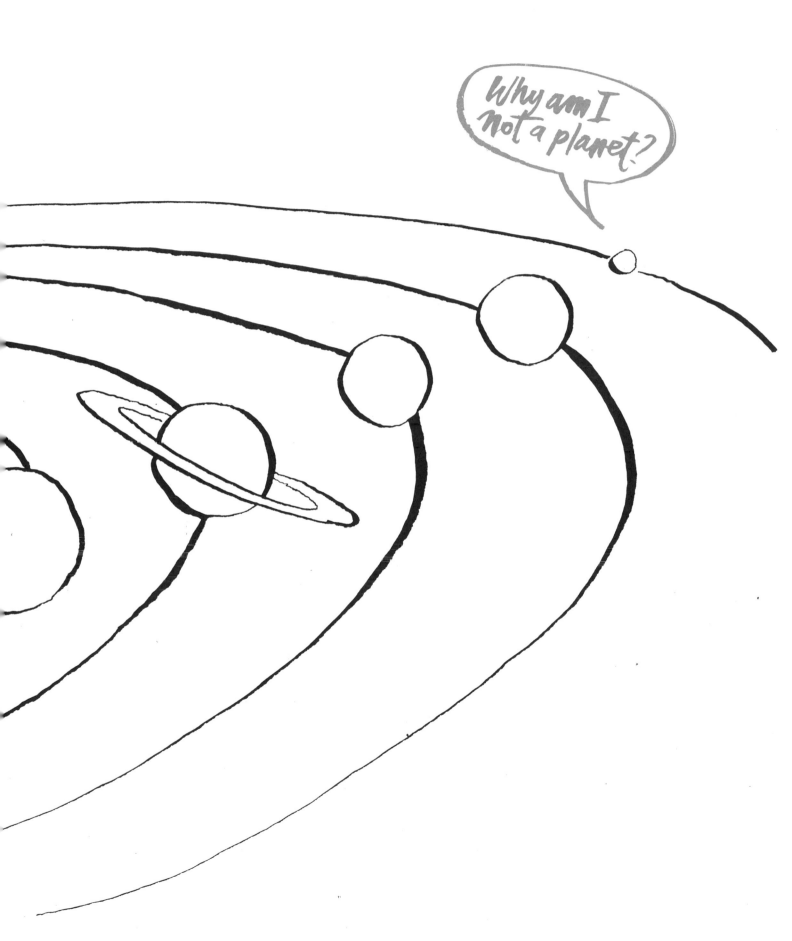

Moons

These are all the moons of the various planets. Close this book and see if you can remember the names of Jupiter's four moons.

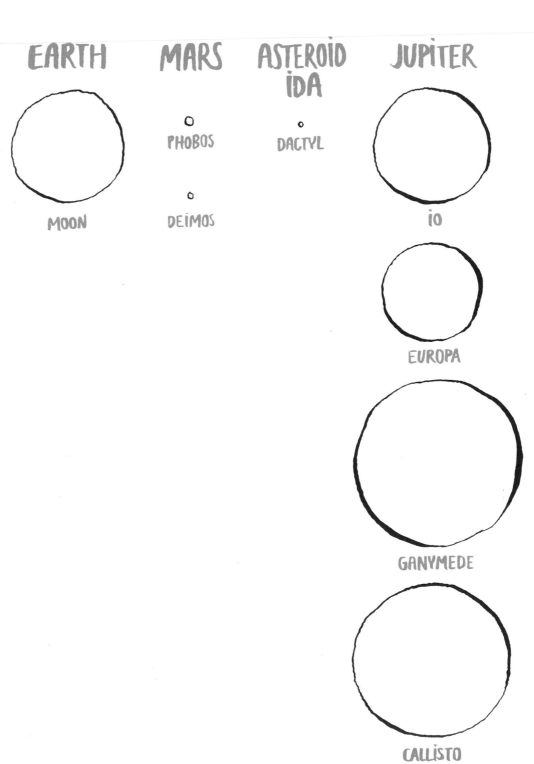

EARTH	MARS	ASTEROID IDA	JUPITER

MOON

PHOBOS

DEIMOS

DACTYL

IO

EUROPA

GANYMEDE

CALLISTO

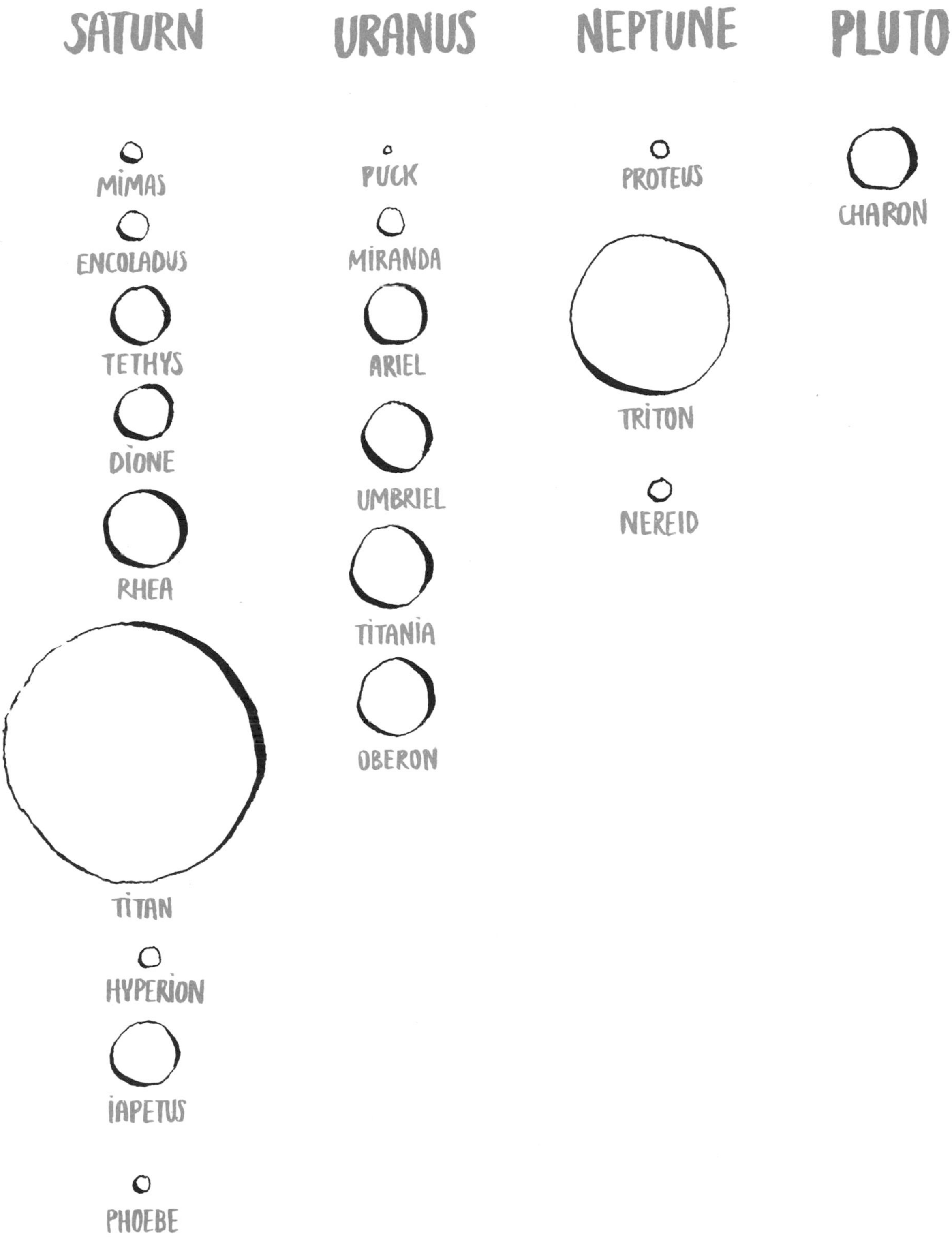

SATURN

○ MIMAS

○ ENCOLADUS

○ TETHYS

○ DIONE

○ RHEA

○ TITAN

○ HYPERION

○ IAPETUS

○ PHOEBE

URANUS

○ PUCK

○ MIRANDA

○ ARIEL

○ UMBRIEL

○ TITANIA

○ OBERON

NEPTUNE

○ PROTEUS

○ TRITON

○ NEREID

PLUTO

○ CHARON

Constellations

Thousands of years ago astronomers identified groups of stars that made shapes resembling people, animals and objects.

These are the constellations you can see in the Northern Hemisphere in summer.

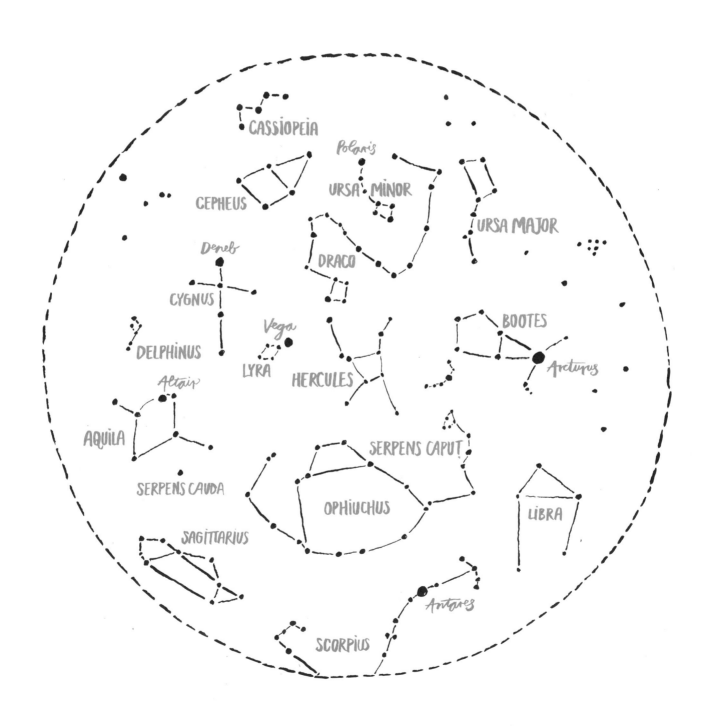

These are the constellations you can see in the Southern Hemisphere.

The Southern Hemisphere is best for stargazing. You can see many more constellations and the Milky Way is more clearly visible.

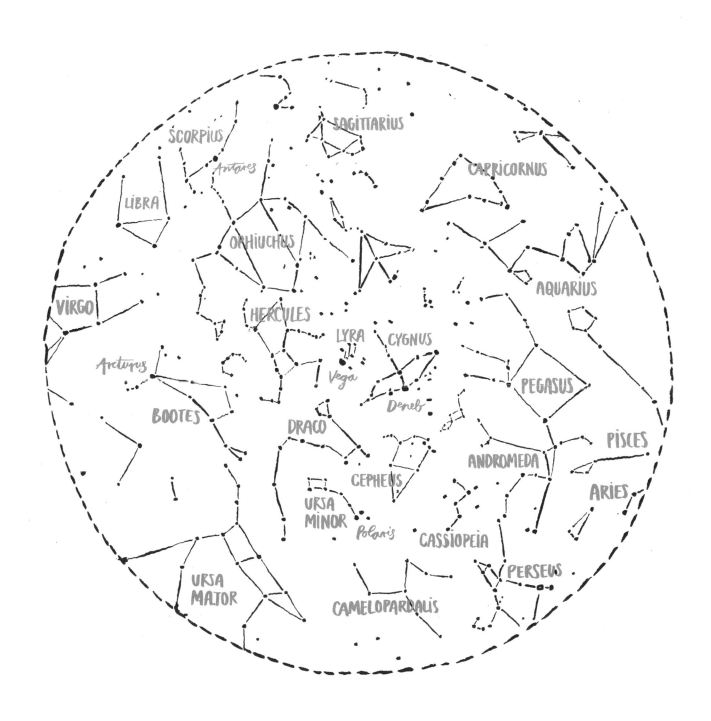

Constellations

Libra represents the scales
of justice – this is how
the stars 'connect' to
resemble scales.

Can you draw the images
around these constellations?

Libra
THE SCALES

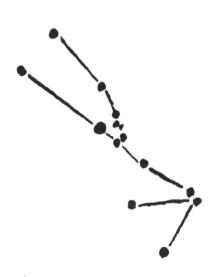

Taurus
THE BULL

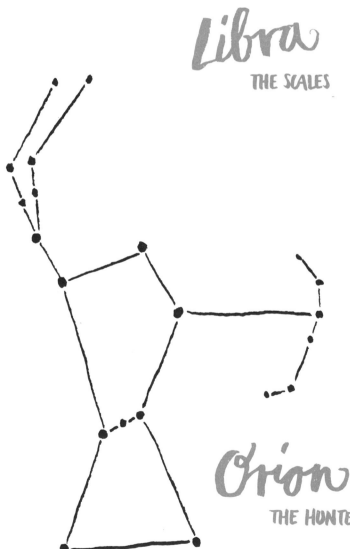

Orion
THE HUNTER

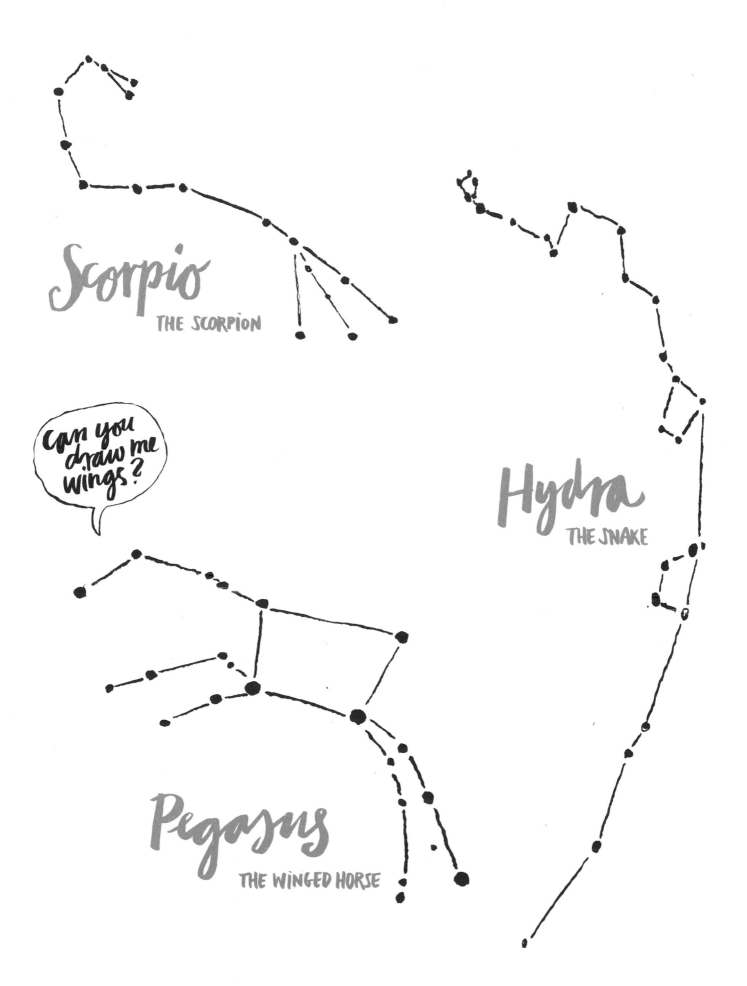

Spacefacts!

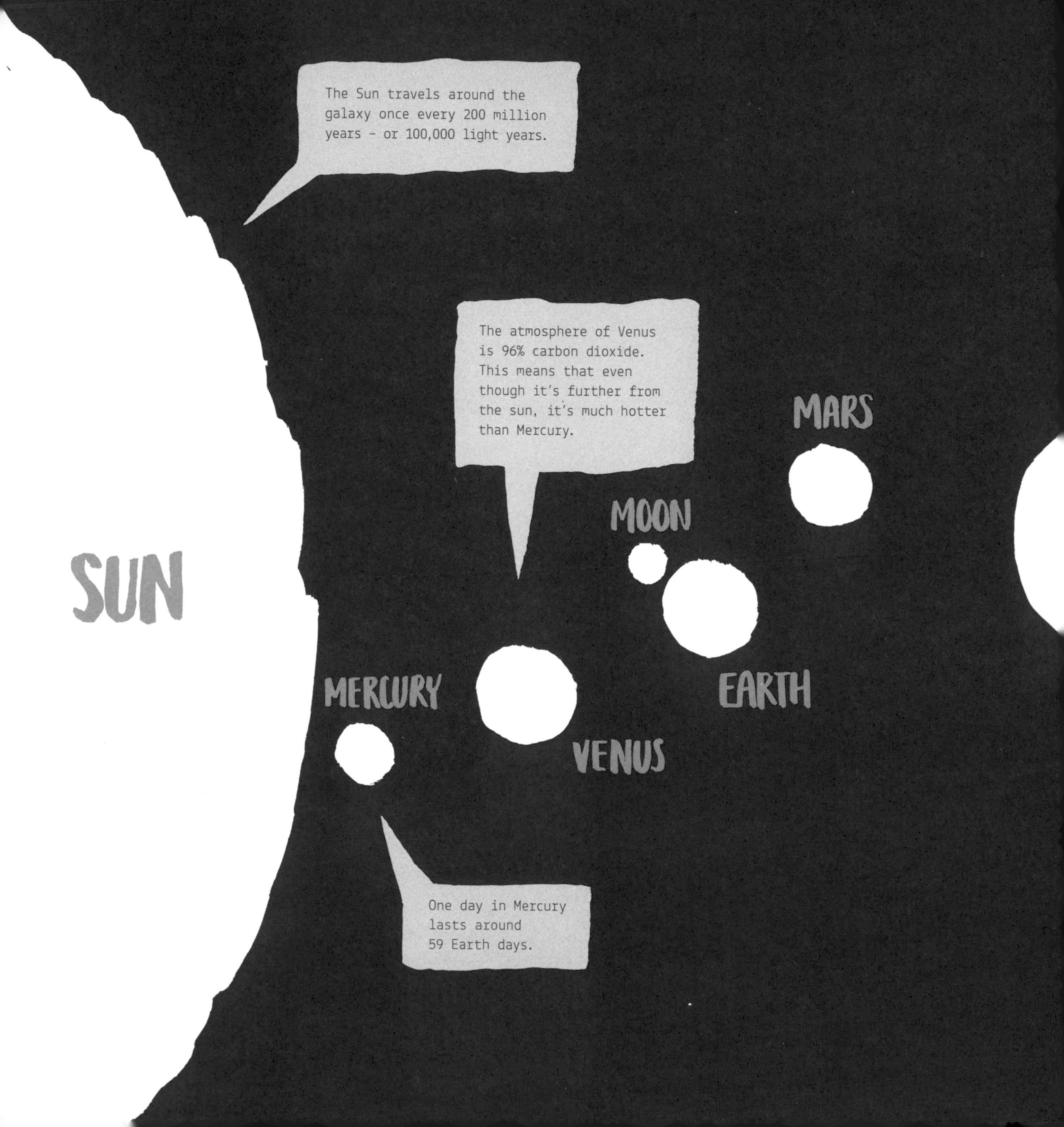

The Sun travels around the galaxy once every 200 million years - or 100,000 light years.

The atmosphere of Venus is 96% carbon dioxide. This means that even though it's further from the sun, it's much hotter than Mercury.

MARS

MOON

SUN

MERCURY

EARTH

VENUS

One day in Mercury lasts around 59 Earth days.

Pluto was once considered the ninth planet in our solar system. It is much smaller than the others, and after finding other icy bodies of similar size that orbit the sun, astronomers decided that it (and the other bodies) should be considered a 'dwarf planet' instead.

Saturn is almost entirely made of hydrogen and helium gasses. Only a small core of the planet is made of solid material.

URANUS

NEPTUNE

PLUTO

SATURN

JUPITER

On Uranus, the summer lasts 20 years, and so does the winter. In autumn, the sun rises and sets every nine hours.

The gravity on Jupiter is 2.5 that of the gravity on earth.

Spaceship

NASA's Space Shuttle is the world's first reusable aircraft. The Orbiter launches from two rocket boosters that blast it out of the Earth's atmosphere.

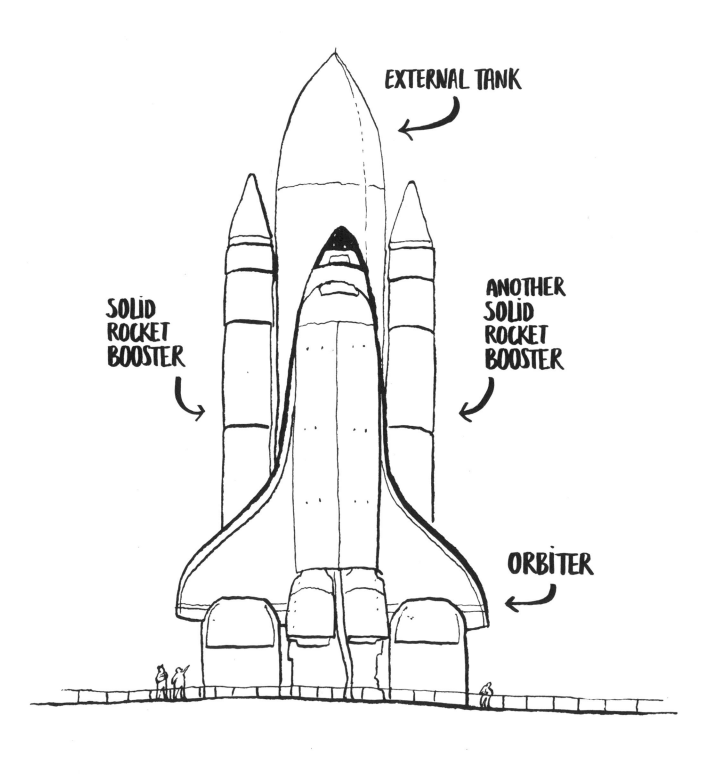

EXTERNAL TANK

SOLID ROCKET BOOSTER

ANOTHER SOLID ROCKET BOOSTER

ORBITER

Design a spaceship
to take you to
strange new worlds!

My Planet

Draw an imaginary planet –
who do you think lives there?

Published by Cicada Books Limited

Illustrated and designed
by Kathrin Jacobsen
Text by Robin Jacobs

British Library
Cataloguing-in-Publication Data.

A CIP record for this book
is available from the British Library.
ISBN: 978-1-908714-20-6

© 2015 Cicada Books Limited

Cicada Books Limited
48 Burghley Road
London
NW5 1UE

T: +44 207 209 2259
E: ziggy@cicadabooks.co.uk
W: www.cicadabooks.co.uk